LIVING WATER

Counselling And Psychotherapy
For Beginners
And Life Skills For Everyone

Judith Schuepfer-Griffin

Psychotherapeutic Counsellor reg. MBACP

*For P., my ever supportive husband and best friend;
for my inspirational friend and colleague Andrew Jamieson;
for my wise elders and teachers Suzanne Trevains and Matthew Harwood
… and in honour of Carl Gustav Jung.*

CONTENTS

Thank You!

Thank you to my friend and colleague, psychotherapist Caroline Le Vine, for reading the manuscript with a keen eye for detail, looking out for lack of clarity, and metaphors gone haywire. Your feedback was truly invaluable!

Thank you to those clients of mine who've read the book and gave me honest feedback from their perspective.

Thank you to my husband P., for your endless support through the decades, for speaking your mind and being yourself, for engaging with me in this challenging, demanding and exhilarating adventure called marriage, and most of all, for loving me.

Thank you to my sister Maria, who was, is, and always will be, my companion on this path. Thank you for your love and support, for challenging me and disagreeing with me at times, for sharing your sparkling creative thinking-power, and your unique view of life and the world.

Thank you to my mother Luisa, for your always curious and open mind and open heart, for your unconventional, always evolving philosophy of life, and for your love.

Thank you to my friend and colleague, psychotherapist Andrew Jamieson, for our inspiring and stimulating conversations through the years about Jungian psychology, and for your passion and enthusiasm for our work.

Thank you to psychotherapist Suzanne Trevains and Jungian analyst Matthew Harwood, for countless enlightening conversations, for your support, and your wisdom. You are my teachers and soul guides.

Thank you to all my clients past and present, for trusting me and working with me. It was and is my honour and privilege; I'm learning so much from you!

Thank you to my therapists past and present, for your guidance, for your emotional presence, for helping me to get to know myself ever deeper, and for teaching me how to live well.

Thank you to all my friends and family, colleagues and students, for sometimes gentle, sometimes energetic, authentic conversations and debates, for listening and speaking up, for sticking with me through highs and lows, for being in my life.

Thank you all, from the bottom of my heart.

Declaration

Some of the chapters in this book have previously been published on www.counselling-directory.org.uk but have since been re-written and expanded by me, to a lesser or greater extent.

"What hurts the soul? To live without tasting the water of its own essence."
Jalāl ad-Dīn Muhammad Rūmī (1207 – 1273)

"[...] And let him that is thirsty come. And whoever will, let him take the water of life freely."
Book of Revelations, 22.17

"Living Water….I love it!"
S.H.

My understanding of "Living Water": the knowledge, insight, understanding and wisdom we can discover and re-discover in order to live a good, creative, meaningful, and fulfilling life.

About The Author

Judith Schuepfer-Griffin completed her first therapeutic training in Transactional Analysis (TA) in 1980 in Switzerland. She ran TA workshops, worked in adult education and many other areas, and eventually found her way into the world of journalism in which she worked for 15 years.

In her early thirties she studied Law at the University of Fribourg, Switzerland, and after having moved to Great Britain, she fulfilled an old dream of hers by studying Fine Art at Bath Spa University College where she earned her BA (Hons) degree.

Eventually, she did further training as a therapist and achieved her CPCAB Level 5 Diploma in Psychotherapeutic Counselling.

At present she lives with her husband on a farm in Bath, UK, and works as a writer, a psychotherapeutic counsellor and supervisor in private practice, as a trainer of counselling students at Sweet Track Centre in Glastonbury, and is running, together with colleagues, Jungian workshops in Bath. She is a registered member of the British Association of Counsellors and Psychotherapists BACP.

Welcome

Dear Reader

Welcome to my book **Living Water**! It contains a collection of articles that I have published over the years in order to make counselling and psychotherapy concepts more accessible. I see it as an important part of my work as a therapist to translate potentially difficult psychological and philosophical concepts into a language that can be understood by everyone. Some of these concepts are in my view so inspiring, exciting and helpful that I want to liberate them from the ivory tower of academia and make them available to whoever is interested, whoever is "thirsty for the Living Water". In an often harsh, materialistic, and increasingly soulless world, we all need more Living Water, more insight into what it means to be human, and wisdom that helps us to live well.

When people are thinking about starting therapy, they often don't know what to expect, and are sometimes a little intimidated or confused when asked to examine their understanding of themselves and of people in general, their feeling and thinking, their beliefs and attitudes, or some of the values of their respective culture.

This book is intended to be a starting point. It is designed to help you to find a way in; to give you practical ideas, alternative ways of relating to others, yourself, your difficulties and your troublesome emotions; new ways of understanding what you perceive as your problems, and how to see them in a different light.

The basic question is: What makes us humans tick, and what is going on when we don't tick so well? – You may have gone through difficult, painful or even traumatic experiences in your childhood or adult life, that, unprocessed, are now hampering your personal and/or professional development, and hinder your attempts to create a fulfilling and meaningful life.

You may experience a lot of pressure from your culture or society to *be* a certain way, to live your life a certain way. If these expectations collide with who you really are, with your true innate nature, an inner conflict will result, that most likely will cause you self-doubt and anxiety; it can make you feel depressed, sad, fearful, or angry. It can make you feel inferior and inadequate. It can cause a lack of self-worth and self-confidence, and difficulties in your relationships.

It's about finding out who you really are, and how you can live your life without suppressing your true nature. Hopefully you will find new inspiration in this book! It is made up of stepping stones that might help you to ease into counselling or psychotherapy with more clarity about what to expect, what you want to achieve and how you could get there.

Or, if you have no intention of going to therapy, it might give you some useful tools to achieve a deeper understanding of yourself, better relationships, a better quality of life and emotional well-being.

This book doesn't claim to be comprehensive, or to contain "the truth". My intention is, to encourage you to find your own truth. I'm merely describing my view and understanding of certain life-questions to which I have come through decades of work on myself, and as a therapist. It's always a work in progress; my understanding constantly evolves and develops, as I do as a person; as we all do as persons.

You may notice that I repeat myself here and there in this book. That's what we also do in therapy: We repeat certain ideas and concepts until they start to sink in and take root. As they say: The longest journey is the one from the head to the heart.

I hope you will enjoy reading this book; that some puzzling life experiences and difficulties might become clearer and begin to make more sense, and that you will feel inspired to make positive changes in your life.

With my heartfelt best wishes,
Judith

PART I

LET US BEGIN

"Most people go through their whole lives
without answering their own questions:
What am I, what do I have within me?
The big stuff. What a waste."

Raynor Winn

1

May I Introduce Myself?

I was born in Switzerland in 1959 and grew up in a small farming village. My childhood, like that of so many others, was rather challenging at times, which led me quite early in life to try and understand what was happening to me, and in my family, and why things were sometimes so arduous and confusing. When I was thirteen, I secretly read a book forbidden to me by my mother who feared that I would lose my Catholic faith if I were to stray from the "right path". Although, thinking about it now, she, a devout Catholic all her life but always remarkably open-minded, must have been looking for new inspiration as well... The book was called *The Three Pillars of Zen* by Philip Kapleau. I never became a Zen Buddhist, but that book is still in my library today; I kept it because it signified an important change in my young life: I decided to find my own way, secretly at first; a way that would work better for me than the one I was taught.

From then onwards I was searching for something, I wasn't sure what, something that would make sense and bring meaning to my early difficult and at times painful experiences. At the age of eighteen I experienced group therapy for the first time, which was a revelation to me. I then stumbled on some Personal Growth workshops which were popular in the 70s and 80s, and which opened up a new world for me. Although I had hardly any money, I did find a way to keep going to these workshops: I worked as a workshop assistant for several years while doing all manner of jobs to make a living. I met people there, amongst participants as well as the course leaders, that understood me, and I them. They spoke my emotional language. It was my first experience of "coming home", of finding my kind of people and my path – or at least the beginning of it. Some of those people are still very dear friends of mine today, more than forty years later.

It was around that time that I also discovered Carl Gustav Jung, the great Swiss psychologist who is, along with Sigmund Freud, one of the founding fathers of modern psychotherapy. Someone gave me Jung's autobiography as a present; it turned out to be much more than a present; it was one of the greatest and most important gifts I was ever given. It changed everything for me; I was hooked. Jung is still today my greatest inspiration for my work as a therapist.

Looking back, it is clear to me that I didn't understand much of what I read then, but nevertheless it excited me deeply and made my heart race. Part of me knew already then, that I had discovered something immensely important.

Jung's legacy is simply colossal. It is so extensive and so many-layered, that a life time is not enough to grasp it all. However, despite of all that he discovered and that we're still trying to understand today, at the end of his life he still thought that his findings "wouldn't even cover the nail of his little finger" (Jung) compared to what there still is to be learned and understood about the realm of the psyche, the soul.

Although I found it quite difficult to find a way in into Jung's work, I kept trying, and eventually some things began to make sense. I helped myself by reading "Jungians", authors inspired by Jung and/or trained in Jungian psychology, rather than Jung himself, until I was ready to tackle Jung's Collected Works themselves.

At around the age of twenty-four I started to go to therapy. I was very lucky! My first therapist was a wonderful, warm and wise human being, and I will be grateful to him for the rest of my life. Since then I always kept on going to therapy, with a two- or three-year gap here and there. Being a client and keeping on digging, searching and questing (while always finding) was one of the most important parts of my training as a therapist. I think this is because I learned so much about myself, and how it feels to be in the client's chair. It was a way of learning by experience, rather than from mainly reading text books. I'm sure I could live without going to therapy now, but why should I? It has become much more than therapy in the narrow sense of the word; it has become my spiritual practice. Once a week I check in with myself in the presence of another human being, a wise elder, a soul guide. In the past we were supposed to be provided with this experience by religions and priests, or their equivalent. Today, this set-up doesn't seem to work anymore for many of us, and we're looking for something that *really* resonates with us. For me, one way of doing this is to see my Jungian therapist once a week.

I've enjoyed studying to be a therapist immensely, but it was in my own therapy that I mostly learned to face myself, my deepest fears, rage, pain and sadness; where I found sense and meaning, joy and fulfilment, and – following my own excited and never ending curiosity – where I learned ever more about who I really am.

"The truth will set you free" and "Know thyself!" are unavoidable imperatives in good therapy (I will use the term "therapy" and "therapist" in this book, rather than the cumbersome "counselling and psychotherapy" or "counsellors and psychotherapists", also because trainings, qualifications and professional titles are different in each country). A therapist can only take a client as far or as deep as they are willing to go themselves in their own self-exploration. That's why, in my view, it's so important that therapists have extensive experience of therapy themselves.

In 2015 I also started to offer workshops here on our farm, mostly for therapists and trainees. At present, we – my friend and colleague, psychotherapist Andrew Jamieson and myself – offer a two-day workshop "Introduction to C. G. Jung" each year, where we look at Jung's main psychological concepts, and two one-day follow-up workshops per year, where we explore one specific Jungian concept at a time in more depth.

I'm enjoying my work immensely, and out of this work has grown my wish to make therapeutic thinking and understanding more accessible to everyone. I hope that in this book you will find some useful and helpful material that you can apply in your own life.

And my path? – It is, and always was, a meandering, crooked kind of path, sometimes hardly visible, leading through wilderness and thorny thicket, sometimes suddenly opening up to great beauty, then almost disappearing again in the undergrowth, no sign posts anywhere, my only guide: my own curiosity and deep need to keep exploring, searching, finding, loosing, re-searching and finding again. It's an endless path, with direction only coming from within, and with no final destination. As I walk it, I create it. It is the path of Who I Am and Who I Am Meant To Become. The path of my destiny.

2

My Core Convictions

As A Therapist

My present core convictions (they tend to evolve) as a therapist mostly formed quite late in my life, but I do remember that I noticed quite early on, maybe around the age of eight or so, that I secretly questioned things and couldn't believe in things that made no sense to me, and that I didn't even *try* to believe in them (e.g. parts of my deeply Catholic upbringing). I carried questions around with me for decades, without finding answers to them. **It is a core conviction of mine to leave questions open and live with them** until they are answered – if ever – in ways that really resonate with me and click into place.

Another thing that I realised quite early on was that, **if I'm not true to my inner nature, things will go wrong**. I tried again and again to fit in, to be and live like others around me, to be and do what was demanded of me, but it frequently went wrong. I got ill, or I just couldn't sustain it. I knew even in my twenties, that my inner nature was very strong, and very strict with me, and that it backfired if I strayed. I noticed this before I had any clear knowledge or understanding of "psychology". I called it "my inner nature" because I didn't know what else to call it. I noticed that it didn't come from the conscious "me" (ego); that it was something different, almost something separate, from deep within.

So my life meandered, didn't go in the straight line prescribed by our culture, from one square box to the next (e.g. school, apprenticeship or university, career, marriage, family etc.) I "stumbled" – or flowed – from one thing to another, found out step by step where I was to go next, what to do or learn next, like a tree grows. **It grows a branch at a time, and from that branch the next one grows.** We don't know what the next branch will look like, and we can't grow straight from a little trunk up to the crown. The crown forms and expands slowly; it develops throughout a lifetime, and a fully matured crown needs to be supported by deep and strong roots, a powerful trunk, and robust branches.

I did sense other potential core convictions within me, earlier in my life, but didn't quite dare to trust them fully; they needed confirmation. This may sound slightly odd, but I'm mentioning it because you might have similar doubts when you hear or sense that quiet inner voice of yours. I started to find that confirmation when I discovered C. G. Jung's work. His comprehensive and inclusive approach spoke to me; I found Soul in his writing, and my whole being responded: It literally did make my heart race. I remember that I bought one condensed volume of his Collected Works a little after I'd read his autobiography, but hardly understood a thing and was deeply frustrated, forever looking for a way in. Somehow I stumbled onto books by Jungians like Clarissa Pinkola Estes's *Women Who Run With The Wolves* which I devoured and did understand, because of her way of using story.

And so it went on, slowly but steadily. Therapy from my mid-twenties onwards helped me enormously to get to know myself, to unpack my unconscious and start to heal my emotional wounds, my repressed traumatic experiences and feelings, but my relationships still didn't work very well. I was looking for what I needed and longed for, in the wrong places: on the outside, in other people. In long-term therapy I learned to look inside of myself, and I realised that my to begin with quite difficult marriage (it goes really rather well now), the relationship I entered into when I was thirty-nine – which was over twenty years ago – was exactly what I needed, in order to make me do the growing-up work that I needed to do. From that experience and the Jungian approach to relationship came the realisation and now core conviction, that **relationships *on the psychological level* are not about making us happy; they are here to challenge everything in us that we buried** and are trying to avoid at any cost. It was Jung who said: "The psyche is not interested in happiness, it is interested in growth." To soften this blow, I would add that inner peace and contentedness, and even some real happiness at times, although not constantly present, will most likely be a by-product of growth, however.

I'm not saying that everybody should stay in their difficult relationships, especially not if the relationships are abusive. **Some couples need to separate in order to allow life to flow again; others, however, could gain a lot by sticking with it, getting help and working things out together.**

This is at the core of my work with clients: **We can't change others, but we *can* change ourselves,** which is at times difficult and painful, but also immensely empowering, healing and liberating.

Which leads me to the question of mental health: In my view this term is often misused and misunderstood. In western cultures, mental health is usually seen as the ability to fit in, to live according to, and to put up with, the enormous pressures of a culture lacking in Soul. People who can't cope, who become depressed, anxious, stressed, angry etc. are seen as having mental health problems. The results of an upbringing that ignores a person's innate nature and tries to mould them and make them fit in too much, are then labelled as "personality disorders", are seen as pathological and are often "treated" by way of chemical substances. I don't agree with this view: Most of us are not ill; we just couldn't find a way yet to be true to ourselves. **If there is the willingness to look at ourselves and take responsibility for our part in our problems, we all can change in ways that will improve our quality of life.**

In *Lord of the Rings*, which I read and watched as an *inner* battle, a psychological process, rather than an outer one, it is said that the first Orcs, the bad monsters, descended from Elves that were tortured so badly, that they turned into what we call Evil. This is an extreme but still helpful illustration of a **destructive development as a result of the abuse, loss, or rejection of one's true inner nature.**

Western culture upholds "rationality", and as a result of this, we worship materialism, achievement, status, image, prestige, logic. **It has become a culture that is out of balance, that is pathological in itself and is psychologically/ spiritually dangerously underdeveloped and ignorant.** Many therapeutic interventions that are designed to uphold these cultural values are as pathological, crude and growth-preventing as the culture itself. So, mental health (!) often appears in the guise of pain, frustration, anger, depression and anxiety.

We perceive these feelings as "the problem", but really they are not the problem; they are *symptoms* which try to tell us that something is going seriously wrong in our lives. **These symptoms are often signs of a healthy psyche that is suffering but is being ignored; a psyche that rebels, and refuses to be shaped and moulded in ways that go against its true nature.**

It's like in the little story of the duck that was told it should (try to) be a squirrel, because squirrels were better than ducks. The duck was very bad at climbing trees and jumping from one branch to another and at collecting nuts, which it didn't even like. When it eventually discovered that it was actually a duck, not a squirrel, it realised that it was brilliant at swimming, diving, and flying, and it became very happy once it manifested its true innate duck-nature (adapted from Rev. Dr. Devorah Greenstein's story, with permission).

I guess I could go as far as to say that this is the core of my core convictions: **All the work I do with clients and on myself is in its essence about recognising, honouring and liberating a person's true innate nature.**

One of the great challenges for clients is often the fact that *their own* core convictions or beliefs may have been "swallowed whole", undigested; learned and adopted unconsciously, and might now be part of their survival strategies and/or defence systems: We all had, to a greater or lesser degree, to make ourselves acceptable to parents and other authority figures in order to survive our childhoods.

Sooner or later we are all confronted with Cinderella's work of sorting the good lentils from the bad ones. We need to sort through our beliefs, values and convictions; to consciously choose what truly serves our personal development, and what needs to be discarded; what is part of our true nature and what is part of our false (or over-adapted) self. Without this sorting-work, we will be unable to "go to the ball" and re-unite with the missing parts of *ourselves* (prince or princess). Myths and fairy tales illustrate these imperative archetypal inner processes that need to take place in all of us, in order to allow psychological growth, maturity and a fulfilling life.

C. G. Jung called this process the Great Work, the Magnum Opus. It's the work of a lifetime, or even more than that: a way of living one's life. It's up to us how we set our priorities: to live an almost exclusively "outer" life and neglect our inner development – or to find a balance of "inner" and "outer" life that will allow us to grow and develop according to our true nature, our innate destiny.

3

The Difference Between Counselling And Psychotherapy

First of all, you might ask, what the difference is between counselling and psychotherapy. In the UK there is no clear-cut answer to this question. In theory, counsellors are dealing with certain issues that may arise in the present, like bereavement, relationship break-up etc. and are often trained in view of working in agencies or charities that offer counselling for a variety of issues, where usually only shorter term therapy is available. But many counsellors work in private practice, deal with a wide range of human difficulties and do deep, long-term as well as shorter term work.

Psychotherapists on the other hand supposedly work on a deeper level, and longer term. However, in practice, this is not always the case. Psychotherapists do also short-term work on specific issues and sometimes refer to themselves as counsellors as well as psychotherapists. Both kinds of therapists may define their ways of working as integrating both counselling and psychotherapy approaches and methods in their practice.

Generally speaking, the different professional titles (which are currently not protected by law in the UK) usually result from different training pathways. Good training is very important indeed, but in the end it's the person themselves that matters, in my view. Studies that were carried out in the US, where therapists train much longer than for example in the UK, came to the conclusion, that the most effective therapists were not those with the longest formal training, but those with the most interpersonal skills and life experience (John McLeod; Therapy Today, April 2018). Which makes complete sense to me, I have to say.

There are some paradoxical sides to the work of a therapist: Yes, we agree to work according to ethical frameworks, rules, regulations, clearly defined professional boundaries and codes of good practice if we are members of a recognised professional organisation. We need to be trained well and know our theory. On the other hand, all the training in the world won't turn us into good therapists, if we don't apply our learning to ourselves as well; if we don't know our own inner depth and don't face up to our own unresolved issues and repressed emotions. So, in the end it's the authenticity and maturity of the therapist as a person that matters, whatever their training, because it's the *quality of the relationship* between therapist and client that is the main healing factor.

If the relationship between you and your therapist doesn't work, the therapy won't work. So, I would recommend that you choose a therapist you feel a connection with, and feel comfortable with, whatever their training background.

4

How It Works

Whether you consider choosing a "Counsellor" or a "Psychotherapist", if you are thinking of going to therapy, you might want to know a bit more about how it actually works. All therapists are different – because they are individual human beings – and work in their own individual ways. This is how I do it: My first personal contact with a potential client happens by phone or email. We then meet for an initial session. For the client, this first meeting is to find out if they feel comfortable with me, and if I work in a way that suits them. For me, this is to find out what brings them here, what their expectations are, whether they've had therapy before, and to explain about confidentiality, cost, duration of sessions, professional boundaries etc.

We then both go away, have a think and a feel, and then decide whether we want to work together. Once we have decided to go ahead, the client will sign an agreement that sets out the framework within which our work will take place. We then will find a time-slot in which we are both free every week. If clients find themselves in the middle of a major crisis, we can meet twice a week until they feel that once a week would be enough. Otherwise we will meet weekly for the foreseeable future. It takes a bit of time to get to know, and connect with, each other. After about six sessions or so, we will review our work together to see what changed since we started, and where we want to go from here.

Some clients want to focus on a certain problem or situation, and once this has changed to their satisfaction, they want to stop. Others might be struggling with an existential crisis and want to go deeper, in which case the work can be open-ended or until the client finds him- or herself on solid ground again and feels, that they want to go it alone from here.

I don't work after one certain method. It's more like having a tool box with lots of different tools in it, and using the one that seems appropriate for this client in this session. Some clients mainly want to talk things through and understand what's actually happening to them. Others have a talent for working with dreams and Active Imagination (a guided process, working with one's imagination); again others might want to learn to communicate in a more effective way to improve their relationships, or how to deal with emotions or experiences that cause them problems, like anger, stress, panic attacks, relationship problems, anxiety or depression, or they suffer from physical symptoms, and body-focussing may be helpful to them.

As persons we are equals, and we are creating this process of change together. It's not for me to tell clients what to do, or to give them all the answers. Their Inner Self, their psyche, knows what needs to happen in order to make their lives better and more fulfilling. Through this process, the answers will emerge from within. It's all there! The treasure lies within *you*. Together, you and your therapist can find out how to unearth it.

5

Where Shall I Begin...

Starting therapy can be quite a challenge; for most people anyway. You may have thought about it for a long time. You may have thought that it might be a good idea to get some help. You may even have decided that enough is enough, and that tomorrow you will pick up the phone and make an appointment. Maybe it was late at night, and you felt relieved to have come to that decision. But the next morning you said to yourself: "Oh, what's the point? It's not *that* bad; I will muddle through somehow. Others are much worse off than me." Maybe you went through this routine more than once, and every time you talked yourself out of your decision.

Starting therapy can be scary. It may seem like climbing Mount Everest, just to make contact with a therapist: "What will she think of me? Will he judge me or talk down to me? Where would I even begin? I don't even know what's wrong with me. Maybe I should just buy another self-help book." Do these thoughts ring a bell? – The point of this chapter is to reassure you; we all go through this inner battle!

Many people suffer in silent despair, sometimes for years or even decades. If you stepped into my therapy room, I would say: "I understand how difficult this is. But there is no need to be so nervous. I will listen to you, I will respect you, and I will not judge you. This is a safe space, and whatever will be said in this room will remain confidential. Congratulations for making it through the door!"

A good therapist will be aware that you both need a bit of time to get to know each other, and together you can work out what exactly makes you suffer. They will allow you to check them out with no obligations, and if you aren't comfortable with them, you can go and find somebody you do like, without having to justify your decision. It's important to find a therapist you can trust and feel comfortable with. Maybe you have to try several until you find the person that is right for you. Maybe you're lucky and the first one is the right one.

There is nothing wrong with self-help books, they do have their place. The only thing is that they won't help you to break your isolation. You will still sit at home alone with a book in your hands, instead of face to face with a human being that cares.

Having to work it all out on our own, is one of the most unhelpful beliefs our culture has produced. The first step to healing is to tell another person what bothers you. Isolation is not a virtue; it is part of the problem. A good therapist will be there to listen, to talk *with* you, to make suggestions, to give you guidance and some "psycho-education". They will be on this journey with you, and they will support you in finding out what works for YOU. So, be courageous and make that phone call. The rewards of this work can be immense!

PART II

SKILLS, IDEAS AND INSIGHTS ABOUT SOME CHALLENGING LIFE QUESTIONS AND SITUATIONS

"I'd finally come to understand what it had been: a yearning for a way out, when actually what I had wanted to find was a way in."

Cheryl Strayed

The following articles don't have to be read in succession; just pick what interests you right now. Some of them refer to a certain season of the year, like Christmas, spring, or Valentine's Day, or the time of year when I wrote them. However, the point I'm trying to make in them is usually relevant all year round.

TIME FOR CHANGE

"Nothing ever goes away until it has taught us
what we need to know."
Pema Chödrön

6

New Beginnings

January is a strange month. All the excitement of Christmas is over, and a new year begins. It would be wonderful to take January off, to have a rest and ponder our lives. But we need to earn a living and to pay the mortgage as usual. Some might have lost their job recently and would rather go to work than taking a break that was forced on them.

What a strange system we live in, a system that forces us to sell our time and work in order to have food and shelter, basically. Of course some people plunge headlong into this system and turn necessity into ambition: To earn as much money as possible becomes the meaning of their lives. But what for? To buy a bigger house or a more impressive car, so that we can feel that we are "Somebody"? – But do more material goods really make us into "Somebody"? Why do we put so much effort into keeping up appearances? –

Probably mostly because that's how we grew up, that's what we learned.

We were not loved just for *being* in our parents' lives; we had to earn their love, often at a high price. We had to be a certain way and do certain things in order to be acceptable, often at the price of who we really were. We developed a public face, an acceptable face, and sacrificed our real self in the process. Alcohol and drug problems, anxiety and depression are on the rise. There are a lot of unhappy people that try to fit into a system that crushes their souls. The system will probably not change much, but *we* can change, ourselves and our lives.

The first step: to take our sadness, emptiness or desperation seriously, to stop hiding it and to start being honest about it, to ourselves first, and then to another person that will listen, and not tell us to pull ourselves together and get on with it.

The next step: to ask ourselves what we really need in order to live a better, happier life. What people usually say when asked this question is: more time to myself, or: somebody to talk to in an honest way. These seem to be small things, but they can be the first steps on a new journey. Make a date with yourself, put it into your diary and make sure that you keep it. Start with an hour a week. You may just sit down with a cup of tea and watch the birds in the garden. Next week you might want to meet a trusted friend for coffee in town. Be honest to them; tell them how you really are. Stop pretending you're okay when you're not. You will be surprised what a difference this can make. Or you may decide to go to therapy. To see a therapist doesn't mean you're mad or ill. It means that you start to look after yourself better. There is no shame in seeing a medical doctor for a physical problem; so why would there be shame in seeing somebody to help you looking after your mind and soul? – You are allowed to take better care of yourself!

7

Now Is The Time!

A good therapist provides a safe and confidential space for people who would like to look at certain difficulties, and to improve the quality of their lives. They might offer short-term and longer term therapy. Short-term therapy could be about six to twelve sessions long, for example for people who have lost a loved one or who have to deal with a lot of change in their lives, like relationship break-down, divorce, children leaving home, or who generally feel that they need to re-orientate and set new priorities. Of course this process can always be extended if needed.

Longer term therapy can include all these issues but could also be focused on personal development and the realisation of a person's unlived potential. It's for people who would like to explore their own depth, to deal with severe trauma, to free their life energy and creativity by working with dreams and images, by looking at physical aches and pains, by developing their spirituality and "making meaning" of seemingly meaningless, upsetting experiences. It's up to each person how deep they want to go, how curious they are about the "mysteries of life".

Some people just want to work on a certain difficulty, others want to go further and explore their inner unknown universe. This can be painful at times, especially when dealing with trauma, but can also be wonderful, enriching and liberating. It's about healing old wounds and about unearthing our inner treasures.

This makes me think of a quote I love: "If I am not for myself then who will be for me? But if I am only for myself, what am I? – And if not now, when?" (Hillel the Elder)

I think this quote comprises everything we need to know about being human, living with other human beings: The first task in life is to look after myself, to take responsibility for myself and my life. If I don't take care of myself, who will? Do I expect others to do it for me? And do they? – I think these expectations cause a lot of pain and misery, because they set us up for disappointment and make us feel dependent and powerless. But "if I am for myself", then I take responsibility for myself and my needs, and I take the power over my life back into my own hands. Besides: What good are we to others if we don't take care of ourselves?

"And if I am only for myself, what am I?" – If I am only for myself, I am isolated, afraid, or hard and bitter, cut off from the world and other human beings. Then I can't experience that we are all connected, that, in the end, we are all One. Then I can't genuinely relate to others and experience real closeness. We are all different, but deep, deep down we are all the same. The same things cause us pain or make us happy.

"And if not now, when?" – Life is not a rehearsal, life is now. If we don't live life now, when will we? – If you want to change your life but don't know how, get help! Good therapy is all about positive change and how to do it: how to change or heal myself; how to allow myself to live a more meaningful and fulfilling life. *Now* is the time!

8

The Past Is Not The Past!

Many people think that therapy is pointless because "the past is the past" and that raking it all up won't make any difference because "it can't be changed". It's the same kind of reasoning that says that there is no point in grieving the loss of a loved one because "it won't bring them back". – Yes, the past is the past, but what we often overlook is that the *effects* of that past are still affecting the present.

That's the only reason why in therapy we do look at the past: to understand – and change – how it affects the present. The point of grieving is not that we hope those tears will bring someone back; it's about getting to terms with and finding meaning in the effects of that loss. The past often holds the key for problems we experience in the present. For example, if a boy learned to be silent as a child and didn't get much attention, then he probably will find it very difficult as a grown man to talk to his partner, to share his thoughts and feelings, because he simply doesn't know how to do it. If he didn't get much attention as a child, he probably won't give much attention to his partner or his own children, or even to himself; he won't know how.

If a girl learns from the start that she is worth less than her brothers, and less important, she will keep feeling this even as a grown woman, maybe mostly unconsciously, and unconsciously she might hand on this lack of self-worth to her daughters. Neglected children – physically or emotionally – often keep neglecting themselves as grown-ups, and sometimes become neglectful or overcompensating parents.

Many people who go to therapy say that their childhood wasn't too bad, kind of normal. But when they look a bit closer, they realise that maybe there wasn't real closeness in their families, that there were no hugs or loving words, that they played alone most of the time, that they were mostly afraid of their parents, and that they thought this was "normal", and maybe still think this today as grown-ups.

When they look even closer at the ways of their parents, grandparents, maybe even further back, they begin to realise that this distance and coldness was handed down from generation to generation, and that they're doing it again, right now, to their own children. They may feel empty, lonely, anxious, depressed or angry, but it never occurred to them that these feelings might have something to do with the way they grew up. We can break this destructive chain and create a better life for ourselves and for future generations. What responsibility and power we hold in our hands! Let's use them for the good!

9

The Journey

Modern-day life is all about achievements, solutions and how to fix things. However, it becomes problematic when we approach our *inner life* with this attitude: "I'm feeling anxious, depressed or angry, or I have relationship problems etc. – What is the solution, how can it be fixed?" The therapist is sometimes seen a bit like a mechanic, expected to turn a few screws, fine-tune some frequencies, adjust a few bits and pieces, so that we will function properly and without disturbances again. We're all solution-orientated and this can work to a degree, but chances are that we might miss the point.

Good therapy is about a *process* that results in change, not primarily about "solutions". And: Therapy is about relating. If the relationship between client and therapist isn't working, if there is no proper connection between the two, the therapy won't work, even if the client is willing and the therapist highly qualified. Every single problem that is brought to therapy has to do with relating, in one way or another. And relating is a process, not an achievement or a solution.

Relationships can't be fixed by finding THE solution. All relationships need patience, sometimes endurance, stamina; they need communication, a lot of input and giving, listening, speaking the truth, showing interest, or sometimes putting your foot down. To work on and live in a relationship is like doing house work: It never ends. There is no clean, final solution; it's an ongoing, never ending journey, a process of tending and caring. Sometimes we experience happy spells, sometimes rough patches, sometimes we feel exasperated and think: What's the point? – The point is that living in a relationship (any kind of relationship) changes us. It's like a piece of iron being heated in the fire, then hammered into shape, which sounds painful, I know, and sometimes it IS painful, as you know from your own experience.

Living in a relationship is a process that makes us grow up and mature. So is therapy, if it works. It's a process that changes us, and helps us to discover the unexpected and surprising about ourselves, the healing that comes from within. The process of relating, of therapy, of life, is like a growing tree: It makes branches, and out of those branches others grow, and out of these new ones yet others grow. We can't grow the top branches before we have grown all the others in between. Some relationships are ended when they needn't be (when relationship-work could help to go beyond old patterns of relating); some are continued when they'd better be ended (when they are toxic and destructive; in which case, new life and growth could be facilitated through separation); some are continued and tended to; they deepen and mature, and so do the people within them. Whatever we do, it's all part of the process, the journey, of *life*, which *will* change us, whether we are willing or not. It's the journey that matters. The process IS the solution.

10

The Seed Of Change

Happiness doesn't mean the same thing to everybody. Personally I'm already "happy" when I feel content and peaceful. Cheerfulness is very nice too and comes to me when things are generally going well. Joyful I feel every time a new client calls me to make an appointment; and I feel exhilarated and excited when a client starts to feel better and "happier". Pleasure or delight I might feel for example when I find a new dress that fits me perfectly and makes me feel beautiful, or when I eat a really good banoffee pie (my idea of heaven).

What does happiness mean to you? Have you ever thought about different grades and shades of happiness, big and small? Do you know what would make you feel content, peaceful or even cheerful? Do you even allow yourself to ask these questions? Or is it too scary, because the implications would be too serious? By that I mean: If you let yourself imagine what would make you happier, you might realise that you need to change certain things or situations in your life, and this realisation can sometimes be quite frightening. Do you instead put up with it, grin and bear it, grit your teeth and get on with it?

Some things can't be changed, but we can change the way we feel about them and make peace with them. But maybe we feel trapped in a certain situation, frustrated, unhappy, clueless, even desperate. We might not know what else to do than to bear it and suffer it. We can't see a way out; we don't know how to change it. So we swallow hard, push away the sadness and carry on as usual. We might not even want to talk about it, because "what good can it do to dwell on it" and "talking never changed anything". Well, I beg to differ! Talking about it is the first step towards change, even if we have no clue how that change could happen. It's about allowing ourselves to acknowledge our sorrow by sharing it with a trusted person, about getting it off our chest, about breaking our isolation and loneliness by entrusting it to someone else – not the actual problem, but our feelings about it.

A muted, isolated person is like frozen soil, like a seed kept in a bag. To keep it all in and "get on with it", is stagnation, paradoxically. We endure life without living it. A person who shares their sorrow with somebody else is thawing the frozen soil and is planting the seed, so that things can start to grow, to move and live again. Sharing our sorrow contains the seed of possible change, the seed of inner peace, contentment or even happiness; but as long as we hold it all in, we can't see that possibility. An apple seed contains the potential of a whole apple tree *and* all its future apples, but can we see that from the outside? No, we can't. We have to plant the seed, entrust it to the earth and let it grow. And then we will see! And we will be able to enjoy its fruits for the rest of our lives.

CARING FOR

THE SOUL

"Music in the soul can be heard
by the universe."
Lao Tzu

11

A Little Help For A Friend

"You're so useful!" an elderly friend said to me the other day after I hung a few pictures in her sitting room and connected her new CD player. She said it with a little laugh and slight hesitation, as if one shouldn't use that word in relation to another person. Usually we describe an object as being useful, not a person. And it made me think. I noticed that I was pleased to please her; it was easy for me to do these little jobs, but to her it meant a great deal.

Often people say when they feel bad about themselves: "I feel useless." Evidently it means a lot to us to be of use to others or to be competent in certain areas, and to *be seen and experienced* as useful and competent. I think it's a basic human need. It's one way of connecting with others and to be mirrored back positively by them.

Unhappiness of any kind, including severe depression, is almost always accompanied by isolation and disconnectedness, which makes us feel useless: "There is no point to me, really; no point to my existence. I might just as well not be here at all; it wouldn't make much difference to anybody else." This is depression speaking, in its various degrees from feeling flat and uninterested in anything, to feeling suicidal. It also has another destructive side-effect: Our thoughts circle around ourselves, our own unhappiness, sadness, loneliness. We lose sight of others around us and their needs, big or small. We become unable to believe that we could make a positive difference in other people's lives. We seem to be the needy ones, and we are ashamed of it. We are hiding that shame, which makes our isolation even worse, and there goes the vicious cycle and becomes an endless downward spiral.

If you recognise yourself in this description, go and get help! There is no need to suffer like this, or to be trapped in a seemingly empty existence. To ask for help is the first step out of the prison of isolation. And, if you feel at all able to, to *give* a little help to someone else is another step. It may not seem much, to hold the door for someone else, to stop the car so that a mum or dad with small children may cross the road safely, or to offer a cup of tea to our partner or a friend. All these are little services to others that show that you care, even if you don't feel that sense of care to start with. But it will make another person feel nice for a moment and most importantly: It will make *you* feel nice. There is nothing wrong with doing a little good in order to feel better about ourselves.

Selflessness is usually misunderstood and sentimentalised. We can't be genuinely selfless if there is no sense of self. So maybe you might want to try this as a small experiment: Do a little thing for someone else once or twice a day and see what happens. It might just bring a small revelation! It's not really about others liking you better; *you* will like *You* a little better. And while you're at it: Go and get help! You absolutely deserve it!

12

The Little Square Box

Your emotions are you; your thoughts probably not. I see a big question mark on your imaginary face: "What is she on about?" – Let's take a closer look: For example, if you feel angry (or sad, scared, anxious, depressed, etc.) a lot of the time you might think that you shouldn't feel like this, that you should be kinder, more patient, happier, nicer, so that you can fit in with society more smoothly. You might think that there is something wrong with you.

While all this is going on in your mind, you probably believe that these thoughts are coming from you, and that your so-called bad feelings are a kind of alien intruder, something that shouldn't be there. – What if you've got it the wrong way around? What if your emotions are coming from the real you, and what you think (what kind of person you *should* be, or that you *shouldn't* feel what you feel) is coming from outside? What if your thoughts are the alien intruders? What we think, or how we think, is usually planted into our minds from the start of our lives. Parents and other authority figures let us constantly know in many different ways how we should or shouldn't be, what we should or shouldn't feel, how we should or shouldn't behave. Some of this is okay to a certain degree, so that we will be able to exist and function in society; it depends how these guidelines are delivered to us. Guidance is okay if it isn't crushing who we are. But if we are getting too many "shoulds" and "shouldn'ts", we won't be able to develop according to our innermost self, the person we are by our innate nature.

This will cause a reaction from our innermost self: If it feels suffocated and crushed, it will react with anger, sadness, fear or anxiety etc. So, if I feel angry a lot of the time, my innermost self is trying to tell me something: "This is not who I really am, you don't hear me or see me, you don't listen to me, and this makes me so angry!" But because we are brainwashed into dismissing our feelings, we will often side with our thoughts instead, the thoughts that say: Don't be stupid! You have no reason to be angry, it's bad to be angry. DON'T BE ANGRY! Which only makes it worse.

As we were forced to fit into a little square box when we grew up, we now keep doing the same thing to ourselves. We keep trying to force ourselves into the little square box. We don't listen to that inner voice that keeps trying to tell us, that things are going very badly indeed for our true nature. The longer we don't listen, the worse we feel. Find a way to claim back your true nature and to learn to listen to yourself again! And find the right help to support you in this!

13

Day *And* Night

"Depression" is a word we all use liberally, for all kinds of feelings and states of mind. Sometimes we may feel down about something, or we may feel sad for very good reasons, like a bereavement or an ended relationship. It's very natural and healthy to feel sad if something like this happens to us; it's not really depression; it's what we *need* to feel in order to go through a process of mourning. If we try to push these feelings away because they are difficult to bear, and painful, or because people tell us to pull ourselves together and get on with it, *then* we might get depressed, stuck, and unable to move on.

"To depress" means: to press or push down, or to pull down. This differentiation is very interesting: If we *press down or push away* difficult or painful feelings, we may become depressed because we try to avoid a necessary and healthy process. The other side of this coin may seem quite alien to us: Our inner self may *pull us down* into a dark place, a black mood, where we feel stuck, trapped, without hope; sometimes over long periods of time: a "Dark Night of the Soul" (Thomas Moore). This could happen because we are too focused on our outer lives and not enough on our inner lives, and because we need to re-evaluate our way of life.

Quite often there are physical symptoms as well: We may feel deeply tired and exhausted a lot of the time; we may suffer from insomnia, from aches and pains, or even from serious, debilitating illnesses. (But: it's of course not as simplistic as that! Sometimes people suffer from serious physical illnesses, and they develop a rich inner life exactly *because* of their illnesses. Their illness becomes their path to self-realisation, as paradoxical as this may sound. Life is still mysterious, and the psyche doesn't work in a mechanical, linear way. I think we need to be careful to respect this mystery.) However, talking about depression: Our inner self often makes normal functioning more and more difficult, because we are ignoring certain things that need our attention. Maybe we had difficult or traumatic experiences in earlier years that still affect us today and need to be acknowledged and digested. Or maybe we are not working on becoming who we could be, who we are meant to be and become, according to our innate nature. The inner self has a plan for us; it wants us to grow and develop as human beings. If we try to avoid this life force, it might seem to turn against us in order to wake us up.

And: Darkness is as much part of life as light. If we try to live "in the light" at all times, we ignore half of our human nature, and darkness will claim its place by pulling us down to it, or by expressing itself through various difficulties. Darkness is not negative; it's the place where germination and gestation of the New happens. We need the night with its stillness and magic as much as we need the day with its light and rationality. Nature shows us on the outside what also happens in our souls: Life is not a straight line; it happens in cycles. Like nature, the soul goes constantly through cycles of germination, creation, fruition and death; or dawn, day, dusk and night. Certain things may need to change or die, so that the next step in our development, the New, can start to emerge. Depression can be awful and debilitating, but it can also guide us in the direction that is right for us – if we really, deeply listen.

14

When The Body Speaks...

In our culture we usually see body and soul as separate entities that have nothing to do with each other. If the body suffers from illness or aches and pains, we go and see our doctor who will normally focus on the symptoms alone, and will treat only that ailing part of our body. There is no time to get to know the person as a whole and the circumstances of their life.

On the other hand, if we have emotional problems of any kind, we either bear them and suffer, and hope that one day it will get better by itself, or we change something in our lives, like find a new job or get a divorce. Or we go and see a therapist who will hopefully help us to get to the root of the problem, so that it won't crop up again in the new job or the next relationship. But usually it doesn't occur to us to go to therapy because of physical problems. We assume that our inner and outer lives are separate, and maybe it never even occurred to us that they might be connected.

There are many physical symptoms that can have emotional roots, like chronic **stomach** problems, indigestion or ulcers. They might say: There is something that I can't digest, that I can't stomach, that makes me sour or bitter. Chronic **back pain** might say: The burden I carry is too heavy, or: I had nobody that strengthened my back when I grew up. **Heart** problems might say: I don't pay attention to my emotions, my heart is blocked up, or: I'm scared of ..., so I'm running away by working, drinking, eating too much, or: My heart is aching, or even broken, because... Chronic **headaches** might say: There is something I carry around with me that "is a total headache". It might be old anger or disappointment that I don't acknowledge, or anxiety that makes me tense up. A **stiff neck** and tight shoulders: Am I generally very anxious; is there fear that sits in my neck? Or: Am I too rigid; do I have too many rules about how things should be, or have to be done? **Insomnia**: What is there that won't let me relax and sleep? What keeps me awake at night? Stiff or aching **joints**: What is it that won't let me move freely, what is paralysing me?

There is old wisdom in everyday language; it's

full of expressions that describe emotional problems by referring to the body. I'm convinced that many aches and pains and chronic or recurring physical illnesses also have an emotional side to them. Unaddressed, traumatic experiences often express themselves through physical symptoms. There is ever more evidence that physical health and well-being can be improved through therapy.

But please don't get hung up on the examples I've given above; they're just an illustration. Each person is unique, and so are the reasons for their symptoms. However, it might be worth a try to give therapy a go. I have seen many times in my work with clients, how physical symptoms disappeared – sometimes immediately and for good – when using body-psychotherapeutic approaches. I have also experienced this on myself. Body, mind and soul are inextricably linked; we are holistic entities and much more than just the sum of our parts.

15

Big Boys Do Cry

The other day I saw a TV programme about men and depression with an alarming prognosis: The World Health Organisation predicts that within a decade depression will be more disabling than cancer. Statistics say that one in four (!) women and one in ten men suffer from it, and it is now assumed, that these statistics may be incomplete, because men often don't talk about it and don't get help, and that there may be a hidden epidemic of depression among men.

They often feel unable to admit to it; they feel stupid, unmanly and pathetic, and that they should be able to "man up" and pull themselves together. They may feel hopeless, and that life is not worth living; they may have trouble sleeping, feel empty or angry and irritable for no particular reason, they may have lost their libido, or their appetite, or eat too much, and they may feel that things will never change. It's like living under a heavy black cloud with no hope of it ever lifting. In our culture, women have more permission to admit that they're unhappy, and women talk more to each other about how they really feel.

Men learn in many ways that "big boys don't cry" and that it is unmanly and weak to cry, or to admit that they are suffering. "Don't be such a wimp," they are told, and usually they are shamed and ridiculed, if they dare to show feelings other than toughness or aggression.

Many men suffer from depression in silence for years or even decades. It may be the loss of their job that triggers a crisis; they feel they lose their identity because they define who they are almost entirely through their work and through being the breadwinner. For others, it may be triggered through an unhappy or failed marriage or relationship. Some men live with depression from their teenage years onwards, after having surrendered to peer-pressure, and the idea, that a real man's life is about working, drinking a lot and being tough.

Depression is often a crisis of meaning. There seems to be no real meaning in many of the things we do. Also professionally and financially successful men (and women) suffer from depression. Our culture is focused on making money and "being somebody" in the eyes of others, but that doesn't guarantee contentedness and well-being.

Our children are pushed hard into occupations and professions that will make them financially secure. But they learn hardly anything about their emotional side, and how to create a *fulfilling* life, rather than focusing only on a financially secure, but maybe quite empty life. We need to take a long hard look at our values and priorities.

Technologically we are a highly evolved culture, but emotionally we are dangerously ignorant and disconnected. We are disconnected from nature, from each other; and from ourselves, our emotions, our needs, our inner lives. Instead of putting our energy into close and meaningful relationships, into understanding who we are and could become *as a person*, or into work that we are passionate about and proud of, and that fulfils us emotionally as well as making us financially secure, we dive into consumerism on every level. We need to start to take this epidemic of depression seriously.

The word "depression" means: "the act of pressing down" and "the state of being pressed down". What are men taught to press down; how are they being pressed down? Did they, and do they still, learn to press down their tears, their sadness and fears, their insecurities and feelings of being inadequate, their inner emptiness and loneliness? – I think they do. – Are they being pressed down by society, by our culture, by our collective demands and expectations towards men, and of what a real man should be like? I think they are.

Studies show that boys are often treated rougher by their parents than girls; that boys learn very early on, to press down their emotions – not only the ones we see as negative, but also expressions of love, tenderness, softness, joy, empathy and compassion.

I think we urgently need to become more aware of, and to re-evaluate, our expectations and treatment of boys. These boys grow into men who have no real access to their more vulnerable feelings and emotions, and so will be prone to aggression and depression. We all – men and women – need a good connection to the whole spectrum of human emotion; it's imperative for mental and emotional well-being. Good therapy can help men who suffer from depression, to reconnect with their *whole* being, and to step away and liberate themselves from emotional gender stereotyping. It will be for their own good, and for the good of us all.

16

When The Volcano Blows...

Anger is an interesting emotion. Unexpressed, it can turn us to stone; unchecked it can turn into aggression and violence, and destroy our lives. What's actually happening when we get angry? – In my experience, it can be like a surge of energy that sometimes makes us lose control. It can be like the eruption of an inner volcano, that swipes away all reason, and it can feel as if we were possessed for a while, spitting out everything that we held in with so much effort.

There are different kinds of anger. We get angry when we witness injustice, when we see somebody abuse a child or an animal, and we want to go and stop them. We get angry at politicians when their decisions seem unreasonable, and we shout at the TV. We get angry if we feel attacked or criticised, when somebody "pushes our buttons", in order to defend ourselves. Anger can also be used to dominate someone else, to bully them, to scare them into submission. Or sometimes we feel overwhelmed; it's all becoming too much, too much pressure at work, too many demands at home, and we finally blow up in desperation and even panic.

We can feel it in our bodies as well: The heart races, adrenalin rushes into our system, the eyes become cold and hard, or they seem to shoot lightning bolts, and we even might want to attack the other person physically, hit them, hurt them or even kill them. It seems to be a primitive energy, that can override all our values and morals, and sometimes we turn into wild animals. I think that anger is connected with our survival instinct and can be healthy and useful; it jolts us into action, it gives us the energy we need to change things, or stop something bad from happening.

But anger can also become a problem. If we try to force our will on somebody else, we're probably not very good at relationships, and this will cause us endless misery. If we suffer in silence until we can't take any more and blow up, we are probably not very good at expressing what we need, and we don't have enough knowledge about how to communicate effectively. If we are very easily hurt or offended, we are probably quite insecure and need to boost our self-confidence and feelings of self-worth. If we like to blame everybody but ourselves if things go wrong, we don't know enough about the concept of "taking responsibility".

A friend once came to me with sparkling eyes and awe on her face and said: "I have discovered the Secret of Life!!! I've realised that I can't blame anybody else, and that I'm one hundred percent responsible for myself! What a liberation! Why has nobody told me this before???" And she grinned at the irony. Anger usually goes with blame; it can be like a Rottweiler out of control, and needs a strong handler: us, ourselves. Anger can be healthy and appropriate, if we learn constructive ways of expressing it. But the more it comes from fear and insecurity or repressed, unbearable inner pain, the more savage it will be in its expression. In this case, we need to respond to, and become aware of, the fear, desperation and pain behind the anger, so that we can find out what we actually need, and how to get it.

That's where therapy comes in. It can help us to learn how to listen to the anger, to let it speak and express itself in a responsible, safe way, without hurting ourselves or others. We need to hear what it has to say, and act on what we hear. Anger can give us a lot of information about what is going wrong in our lives. Maybe it's old anger that we still carry around with us, and we need to work with it. Or it could let us know that we're off track with our way of living, that we have a lot of unmet needs. In this case, we can learn how to deal with these needs, how to take responsibility for them (which means: how to *respond* to them) and how to get them met. Our anger is not the enemy. It could even turn out to be a very valuable friend – if we learn to hear it, understand it, and act on it constructively.

17

What Do You Regret?

Getting older is not easy in a culture that is obsessed with youth. We seem to find it difficult to accept, that our bodies and minds aren't so agile any more, and that we may need a bit of help. We don't only look forwards any more to the goals we aim for; we may start to look back now and then, to see what we've achieved so far. Many people get to middle age and ask themselves: "What now? I have raised my family or built my career, that's all fine; but is this it now?" Or we might have reached old age and may be bored or lonely quite often; maybe our friends are slowly disappearing, passing away, and we are confronted with the fact, that we too will die sooner or later.

If not through early tragedies, it's usually in middle age that death enters into our lives, when our parents die. Then we suddenly realise, that we are now the oldest generation, and that we are next in line to leave this world. This can be quite a shock, and it might bring us back to existential questions: What am I actually doing with my life? Do I spend my days caught up in worries about insignificant things? Do I still have close friends, or have I neglected and then lost sight of them? Do I regularly take time to be on my own and reflect on my life, or do I keep running from one duty to the next?

I think, there isn't one big "Meaning of Life"; it's in our hands to make our lives meaningful to *us, every day*. Getting older and slower has a purpose: It gives us the chance to start looking inwards more often; it's the time to count our blessings and regrets.

There is nothing wrong with having regrets; it's human, and it's liberating to admit them. Recently I sat with a dying old man. We talked, and I asked him: "Would you do anything differently if you could go back in time?"

"Yes," he said, "I would do *everything* differently."

I was surprised by his answer. How sad, I thought, to have lived a life that leaves him so full of regrets, that he would want to do *everything* differently.

Then I started to feel admiration for this man, for his ability to look this reality fully in the eye, and to admit and accept it. How much courage it must take to be so honest! But how liberating it was for him! He seemed sad, but also relieved. And then he was able to let go, peacefully. But wouldn't it be even better to realise this before we are at death's door, and start to turn our regrets into positive change, so that, whatever time we have left, becomes meaningful to us? – Start now! It's never too late.

18

The Vicious Look In The Mirror

According to various studies 60 to 90 percent of women in the UK hate their bodies, and only three percent are totally happy with the way they look. Aren't these figures shocking? What's going on here? – We all have heard that there is huge media pressure on women, and increasingly on men, to look a certain way. We should all be thin – not only slim but thin – and flawless in every way. Just look at the adverts that bombard us every day, with creams and lotions that should make us look younger, and all the pills and potions that will make us thin, or so they promise.

There are the social media and the fashion magazines, full of skinny girls with endless legs, airbrushed and photoshopped, and not real, but we still fall for it. – Why? – Because we're brainwashed, of course, but I think it goes deeper (as you know, I like *deep*): Most of us feel in many ways that we're just NOT GOOD ENOUGH. We have internalised this message, we believe it. Not thin enough, not beautiful, intelligent, interesting enough, not nice and kind enough, not efficient, talented and educated enough... Some fashion designers, when asked why they use these skinny children as models, say that clothes just look much better on tall, thin girls. But who are these clothes for? – They should be for us, all of us, whatever our shape or size.

Women and girls try to make themselves fit into these clothes that are designed for boyish bodies: tall and skeletal, no breasts, no hips. What *should* happen is that designers look at female bodies lovingly, and make clothes that make us feel good about ourselves. Most of us have internalised that vicious, critical look in the mirror: We see all the things that we don't like or even hate about our bodies. We don't look at ourselves kindly, approvingly, lovingly. It's daily torture. We know that diets don't work, but we still do them. We wear shoes that cause agony, and clothes that pinch and don't fit. We constantly live with this nagging feeling that there is something wrong with us, and *we take it out on our bodies.*

Female bodies are a war zone. Self-hatred expresses itself in how we look at, and treat, our bodies. – Let's stop this! The first step is to become aware of how badly we treat ourselves, and to decide: Enough is enough! Try this: Look in the mirror and say: "My body is fine, and I'm fine the way I am." Start to reject this madness. Look at yourself kindly and with love. Look for the things you *like* about your body. The nasty voice in your head will try to protest; don't let it! Tell it where to go!

Like I said: This is only the first step. There will be many more steps to be taken, depending on the real root causes of your self-hatred, and good therapy can help you with this.

However: Try a little experiment. Try being on *your* side! Consider the possibility that you *are* good enough, just the way you are!

19

The Rivers Of Life

While I'm writing this, the Somerset Levels in the UK have been under water for several weeks now; people and animals had to be evacuated. It's assumed that it got so bad, because the rivers and canals in the area haven't been dredged for far too long. They are full of silt and can't hold enough water to help the floodwater get away. And so, disaster strikes, and everybody is lamenting, even though this outcome was very probable indeed. This reminds me of psychological processes. The psyche needs constant attention and looking after, sometimes more, sometimes less intensely. But if we ignore the psyche and the inner goings on, they will turn against us and we will sooner or later get stuck in the mud. The inner streams and rivers get silted up, and life becomes difficult.

Only recently have we begun to realise, that we need to look after our environment, nature, our resources like water, air, the soil and that, if we don't, we commit slow collective suicide. What we haven't realised yet is, that the same applies to our inner world, the universe of the psyche. If we don't take care of our inner resources, they will stop to nourish us; our inner life-giving rivers will silt up, and emotional flooding will devastate the landscape of our lives: depression, anxiety, anger, relationship problems; empty, meaningless lives will be the result.

We all know the word "psyche", but it's virtually meaningless to most of us. Many of us know nothing about an Inner World and its workings, let alone that it might have an effect on our everyday lives. It's almost like assuming that there can be day without night, that there could be only men in this world but no women, that a living thing should be able to exist without water. It's impossible!

We assume that we should be able to live good lives without ever paying attention to our psyche, our soul, our emotional world within. It's like trying to walk on one leg. There seems to be this intense fear of what we might discover, if we dared to look inside ourselves, and we don't know about the inner treasures we will never discover. Of course we're always on the lookout for these treasures but confuse them with money, image, material things. We don't realise, that we're looking in the wrong places, and that, what we are really looking for, is right there, within ourselves: meaning, fulfilment, love, energy, joy, creativity, inspiration, connectedness.

If we let these inner, potentially life-giving rivers silt up, they will in time flood and devastate our inner landscape, and we might drown in self-doubt, loneliness, sadness, resentment, and too often despair. So let's get those diggers out and clear the river-beds of all the repressed, rejected, ignored and dismissed feelings and emotions, so that the Waters of Life can flow again!

20

The Inner Wall

Many of us grew up in families where one didn't talk about feelings. Maybe it was seen as self-indulgent, or it was just experienced as embarrassing. So we never learned to deal with feelings, especially difficult ones, in a constructive way. They were either acted out through screaming and shouting, through aggressive or even violent behaviour, through harsh words and criticism, or through silence: They were bottled up, repressed, or dismissed.

Maybe we were asked sometimes: "How are you?" and we responded: "Yeah fine, not too bad." Probably nobody ever insisted and said: "No, how are you really? How do you feel? What's on your mind?" – We stay at a safe distance from each other and make sure nobody ever gets too close to how we really feel. This may be the appropriate thing to do in a social situation, but not in a relationship or family. There won't be real closeness if we can't talk to each other about our innermost feelings. Children will then never learn that there are other ways to deal with difficult feelings than acting them out or bottling them up; that the results will be different, if we either act angrily and aggressively, or swallow the anger, or if we say: "This makes me really angry!" and the response would be: "Right, I understand! Do you want to tell me why this makes you angry?" (or sad or scared etc.)

If we are allowed to express our emotions, including the pleasant ones like happiness or excitement, and are heard by someone who really wants to know, we learn to be aware of them and to understand them. We also learn, that to express emotions in this way creates closeness. It's how love comes about. If there is a mountain of unspoken feelings between us, then we lose sight of each other; we feel lonely, and the love we might have felt for the other person at one time, gets buried under a heap of rubble. It's still there, but we can't feel it any more. If instead we learn to speak and to listen to one another, then love will come back.

This is of course not as easy as it sounds. If it feels dangerous to speak about feelings, if we are scared to be rejected or humiliated, then that is probably what happened to us in our childhood. We learned to build defences, like an inner wall, that protected us from hurt. But later, this inner wall will get in the way; it won't allow us to be really close to someone else. We might still long for closeness, but at the same time we won't let anybody come close, and we'll push them away without even realising it. Good therapy can help you to take the inner wall down, brick by brick, and to bring love back into your life.

21

Taboo

Even in our supposedly liberal culture, there are still things we find impossible to talk about, or even to admit to ourselves. One of them is the fact that we sometimes feel relieved when a partner, spouse or a parent dies. We feel that we should be sad, or at least be *seen* to be sad when an unloved family member passes away. If we secretly do feel relieved, we usually feel very guilty about it. It's not allowed, not acceptable. "Do not speak ill of the dead!" we learn.

Why is that? Because if we do, they might haunt us? This could be one possible, unconscious fear. – Or is it because so many who live in unhappy families or relationships still do everything to keep up appearances, because they feel ashamed and embarrassed? The collective expectation is still, that we live in happy families and relationships, even if reality is so different. An old friend of mine who allowed me to tell this story, had a very difficult relationship with her father who was a violent and volatile alcoholic. She grew up in fear and never knew what disaster was going to happen next. She left home very young, and after many years felt that she was over it and had forgiven her father. But when he died, she didn't feel loss, but huge relief. She realised that her whole life she had been waiting for this day. The night before the funeral she couldn't sleep and noticed, that all the old anger and hurt was surfacing again.

Unexpected words formed in her mind, saying: "If there is a heaven, and you are in that heaven, then I will never want to be in that same heaven with you! I never want to see you again in all eternity!" She was shocked and surprised by this, and she realised that she hadn't made her peace with her father after all. At the funeral she shed some tears, but not tears of sadness, but tears of rage. After the funeral she went home and called a therapist to help her to work through, and get to terms with, her overwhelming anger and hurt that she still carried.

In therapy, she finally felt able to express what she really felt, without being judged or condemned. She learned that there was no need to feel guilty about her feelings, and that to acknowledge and express her anger, her pain, and her grief for what she never had in her relationship with her father (love, warmth, security, encouragement, praise, play, laughter), slowly healed the wound in her heart. She emerged from the process with new energy, zest for life and peace of heart. Finally, her father didn't haunt her any more.

22

Spending Time Alone

Spending time alone is not everybody's cup of tea. Some crave it, some hate it. Being alone is most difficult for people who are not at ease with themselves. There may be too much noise in their heads, too much inner conflict and debate, too much insecurity or fear. If we're dependent on the constant presence of others, there is usually a big black hole inside ourselves, and we start to feel that deep emptiness inside when we're alone. The other side of the coin is often, that our relationships with the people whose presence we crave, is also not great. If we *need* their presence, we probably suck there emotional energy in order to fill our inner emptiness. This might drive them away from us because they can instinctively feel that they are being drained. In short, we can't live with them and we can't live without them.

If this is the case, we really need to work on our

relationship with ourselves. Another person can never fill our inner emptiness, only *we* can do this. If we even feel that another person is our life-blood, our oxygen, then there will be a part of ourselves that is still in its infancy and is really craving to be parented. We may look like a grown-up on the outside, but on the inside there is a baby that is totally dependent. To be able to be alone and enjoy our own company requires a good connection with ourselves and the ability and willingness to take responsibility for our own needs, which means: *to respond* to ourselves. Then, to be alone at times will feed us; it will help us to "regroup" (since we are all made up of many inner parts), to recharge, to feel again who we are and to re-orientate.

It's like being on a long walk, but then to sit down on our own, to rest and reset our inner compass, so that we can figure out where we are, and where to head from here. To be able to be alone at times, and at peace with ourselves, is a grown-up thing. The more securely we are rooted and connected in ourselves, the more at peace we are, whether we're alone or amongst others. To spend time alone can be a wonderfully liberating and nourishing experience. To realise that we don't *need* the constant presence of others, and that we're complete within ourselves, will make us truly able to love, to relate to others in a healthy and enriching way. If we become mature enough to be able to take care of our own needs, the more our love will be about *giving,* to ourselves and to others, instead of *needing from them.* Two of those can make a truly happy couple!

23

Menopause: The Second Spring

Nowadays, old age sets in much later than it used to. To be fifty doesn't feel old anymore; it feels more like midlife, and there is potentially still a lot of life ahead of us. For most women, it is around this age when the body starts to change. Fertility decreases and then ceases; menopause sets in, and with it quite often some difficult physical symptoms like hot flushes, drier skin, weight gain, insomnia, tearfulness for no apparent reason; loss of interest in sexual relations, which affects their relationships and adds more challenges. And, as if this wasn't enough to deal with, there may also be emotional turmoil, depression, mood swings, the feeling that we are not proper women anymore because of the loss of biological fertility.

On top of all this, middle age is also often the time when children become independent. In a nutshell, everything changes. The symptoms of change are different for each woman. Some sail through it with not too many difficulties. Others suffer badly and feel like their whole lives are being turned upside down *and* inside out. They often suffer in silence because "we don't talk about stuff like that". Of course this is not a good tactic. Not only are we affected by all these changes in our innermost intimate self, but everybody around us is affected as well, often without realising what's going on. The more we hide or resist this change, the more problems it will cause. And of course it will not go away, even if we try to ignore the challenges it brings.

This time of life is in Jungian psychology called "Midlife Transition". It is inbuilt in us, not only in our bodies but also in our psyches. It's in our "psychological DNA". A lot depends on our attitudes towards it. It's not called "The Change" for no reason; it's the time in our lives when we *need* to change, when we *need* to learn new ways of looking at life and ourselves. In the far east, menopause is also called "The Second Spring", the time in the life of a woman when the energy rises from the womb to the heart where it deepens her wisdom.

The end of biological fertility is a relief for some women; for others it's a big loss that needs to be grieved, so that they then can move on to a new kind of creativity which is not about biological fertility any more, but about maturity and experience of life, about wisdom, about owning our authority, about handing on our knowledge to others. It's the time of life when we are not simply defined by being mothers, partners or daughters; it's about remembering who we are in ourselves and what we want our purpose to be for the next few decades. If we can gently let go of our roles of the past and look forward to new possibilities of growth and self-development, then The Change can be The Chance, a Second Spring, an opportunity for a see-change. If we change our attitudes, the symptoms often improve, or we can learn better ways of coping with them.

There are many websites that recommend physical exercise of any kind, talking (with our partners, friends, or a therapist), sleep, relaxation, self-pampering, a healthy diet, doing things you enjoy etc. All these activities are about self-care, listening to yourself (your body, mind and heart), about *taking time for yourself*, about doing something for *yourself*. It's a large part of most women's lives to look after other people, in many different ways, and we forget how to look after ourselves, to find the way back to ourselves. Many of us don't even know who they are as an individual. We always knew ourselves in relation to others and their needs. Menopause, the Midlife Transition, is the time to focus more on ourselves and learn what self-care actually means. It's not just bubble baths and a walk now and then. It's about creating a life we don't need to escape from, a life that reflects who we are *now*.

The only way through it is forward; there is no going back. We will never be young again, whether we accept it or not. But why would we want to? This is *Our Time* now!

24

The Change For Men

We easily forget that men, too, go through a midlife change. We often call it the Midlife-Crisis, usually with a bit of a smirk. We might think of men who, mid-life, suddenly leave their wives and "swap them for a younger model", of men who buy a heavy motor bike or a sports car. It's a bit of a cliché and we tend to think of them as lads who don't want to grow up. There might be a little bit of truth in this because men, too, face the challenge of taking the next step in their development: the Midlife Transition. Maybe they have achieved a lot; they are or were successful and earned their money. They are focused on material success and have no clue what should come next at middle age.

We have lost the knowledge about the phases of life, of initiation into the next stage of our personal development. Some middle-aged men start to suffer from depression and say: What now?

I have achieved what I wanted to achieve, yet everything seems meaningless, empty. Is this all I am, a provider, or a "big man in society"? They are totally identified with their work and status, and all they know to do is: going after more of the same: money, power, sex, status, image; but this doesn't cure the emptiness. Jung said that the challenge for men in midlife is to "develop from desirousness to connectedness". It's the process of desire ("I want") maturing into relatedness ("I give and receive"); the energy also rising up to the heart (love and wisdom).

They too, like women, need to grieve the loss of youth and learn to accept it. Getting older is for all of us about becoming more mature, more loving, and wiser; of handing on to younger people what we have learned and experienced. It's about examining our lives, and finding out what we want to do with the rest of it. Maybe for these men it would mean to work a little less, to spend more time with their families and friends, and on their own! Maybe, like women, they should even leave a dead marriage but can't find the courage.

In midlife we all need to learn to look inwards, to discover a whole new universe in there, and to cultivate the neglected garden of the soul. Many men fall into the trap of trying to prove that they're still young and virile, while unconsciously they begin to fear their own mortality but refuse to face up to the fact, that one day they too will die.

I think, to become aware of all this is in a certain sense even more difficult for men than for women. Women are forced by their bodies to confront these issues, while it is not that obvious for men, that a new stage of their lives is beginning. If they try to deny this fact, they may become sick or grumpy old men; bitter, cynical, disappointed. But if they accept the challenge, they could become mature and wise human beings.

What's wrong with learning something new, taking more time for doing something creative, for reading more, for tinkering in the shed, for going fishing, for writing down the story of your life, or volunteering for a cause close to your heart? What's wrong with relaxing in a garden chair now and then, watching the world go by, peaceful and wrinkly, with a knowing smile on your face?

25

Care For Carers

Today, a large amount of people are looking after a member of their immediate or extended family who is ill or old, or both. Some people have to give up their jobs in order to look after someone and are getting financially into dire straits, which will cause huge anxiety by itself.

To look after someone can also be an immense *emotional* strain, especially if the relationship with that person was already difficult before they needed care. Carers may find themselves chained to the house, never being able to go out without organising expensive sitters, and even if they manage to put such an arrangement in place, they still have to be back at home by a certain time, never feeling free to stay out as long as they want to.

A lot of carers are focused on another person 24/7, looking out, listening out, never able to relax and turn the focus on themselves for a while. They start to forget what they need, they don't have an independent life anymore; they live in constant tension and apprehension. Some are too exhausted to even think of respite and how to organise it. This is not only true for private carers; professional carers are in danger of burn-out as well. To be focused on other people's needs all the time is extremely demanding. It is very important to have regular breaks from this work, and to remember your own needs: time on your own – preferably away from the "patient's" living space – a night out, time with friends, a weekend away.

Friends are immensely important. The danger is that we neglect them and let these relationships suffer or fizzle out, or when we do meet with friends, all we talk about is ourselves and our difficult situation, and we forget to show some interest in them and their lives. Even very good friends run out of patience sometimes if we only talk about ourselves; and it's good for us to also hear and talk about other things than our own problems.

Therapy is another possible support. Therapists are here to exclusively listen to *you*; you don't need to worry about them. There are charities and carer centres who offer activities, therapy, and some even holidays, for carers. There are also the therapists in private practice who can be there for you short or longer term, whatever you need. They can help you to remember your own needs, your own life, and maybe how to think more creatively: how to get more support or make more space for yourself, how to better nourish yourself, body, mind and soul, with respite, proper food and fresh air, inspiring conversations, books, films, art or craft etc. Your physical and mental health is important. How about learning to take better care of *yourself* for a change?

26

Detox For The Soul

Many people make New Year's resolutions about doing better in the coming year, in various ways. There are always a lot of resolutions about healthier living, less sweets, more exercise and body detoxification. It's a good thing for sure to try and live healthily, it's just that most of us focus on a physically healthier lifestyle only. We forget – or have never learned – that a psychologically healthier lifestyle might be as important. We now hear more and more voices – of scientists and doctors – saying that the whole detox industry is a mere money-making machine, that the body is perfectly capable of detoxing itself and is doing so all the time. Problems usually occur through overload and imbalance in our nutrition, not because the body isn't equipped to get rid of "toxins".

It's similar with the psyche: We are resilient beings, and our psyche is normally very well equipped to get through rough times and to heal itself. Stuckness and mental health problems usually occur through overload or emotional starvation which both equal imbalance. If there is too much trauma, parts of us freeze, and the mind becomes unable to process the trauma and to heal. If we learn from childhood to eat healthily and to exercise, our bodies will be perfectly capable of detoxing themselves. Maybe we need more soul-detox than body-detox: less stress and noise, a slower life style, more soul food, less quantity (of distractions), more quality (of life).

Whatever we bottle up will probably start to poison us from inside, so: more talking about what bothers us, more connecting with each other which will improve relationships. More openness, less "silent hero", less sulking, more honesty. More listening, to ourselves, our needs and feelings, and to others, whatever they want to share. A simpler lifestyle, less unnecessary financial commitments, a smaller car, less status symbols, more time to ourselves and our families. Less unnecessary shopping, more playing, talking, picnicking, music-making, laughing, walking. More creativity in its many forms, less emotional junk food. More time to do nothing at all.

We are more and more obsessed with looking

young and being physically healthy, yet our general health gets worse; obesity, allergies, dementia etc. are on the increase. Maybe all our obsessing about physical health is – at least partly – an avoidance technique. We avoid checking our values; we become more and more materialistic. We ignore the soul and its needs, in fact we don't even know that we're doing it. All our thinking is focused on money and things, and on a beautiful, never ageing body of course. Well, it's not working! We're not happier or healthier, be that physically or mentally. Maybe it is time for a soul-detox. Maybe we do need an overhaul of what we value most in life. Why not start now?

27

What Keeps You Awake At Night?

Insomnia can be a tricky one. Many of us seem to suffer from it nowadays, and there is no one simple cure for it. I think it depends on the person and their circumstances, and it's about finding out what keeps *you* awake at night. There can be many reasons for it. Some can be physical, like the "night eating syndrome" for example. Some people – like me – wake up in the small hours and are so hungry, that they have to get up and eat something (you can look this up on the Internet).

Menopause can be another cause for sleeplessness. At that time of our lives, our bodies and their workings change constantly, and this may affect our sleep patterns. Sometimes it helps, to calm ourselves and learn to live with it in a more positive way. You could read for a while (maybe in the spare room, so you won't disturb your partner) or write in a journal whatever is on your mind.

I myself have lived with sporadic insomnia since the start of early menopause at the age of forty (now twenty years ago). I sometimes nearly drop off, and then a hot flush kicks in (I've been living with them now for about seventeen years which is a bit unusual) and I'm wide awake again. When this happens, I go to the spare room and read. The surprising thing for me was to realise, once I relaxed about it, that, even if I lost two hours of sleep, I wasn't tired the next day. I now quite enjoy those solitary quiet hours to myself in the middle of the night.

One of the most common sleep-snatchers is anxiety. Unresolved practical problems go round and round in your head; you get tense and can't drop off. Once these problems are sorted out, sleep usually returns.

There is also another kind of anxiety: Its roots are deeper. It could be that you don't pay enough attention to your inner life, your personal needs, and are totally focused on your outer life like family, work etc. and the soul tries to get your attention by keeping you awake, or waking you up, sometimes through dreams. It literally says: "Wake up! Pay attention!" What's needed in this case, is more time for yourself, more reflection on how you live your life. We may think that insomnia is the problem, but it may just be a symptom of something deeper. You may even think that you are depressed because you can't sleep, but often the depression has deeper, unrecognised causes, and once these are addressed, sleep returns.

The most important thing, in my experience, is to stop worrying about sleeping (or not sleeping). I know, this is difficult, but try to go with the flow a bit more: It's not the end of the world, although it may feel like that sometimes. Obsessing about sleeping will make it worse. At the same time: Inform yourself. There are many websites where you can find practical tips, and there are also reports of good results with Cognitive Behavioural Therapy courses (CBT) which mostly focus on attitudes, beliefs, negative thought patterns and helpful strategies.

Stay calm and try them out. If they don't work, you could try deeper therapy. I know, this may sound like a contradiction: to calm ourselves *and* to get help. In therapy, we often don't tackle a problem head-on, because if the problem is a symptom of something else, this would only make it worse. We look at it from all sides, and we look underneath, to see what might be the cause of the symptom. In any case, once your soul has your attention, it may let you sleep again.

28

Sweet Dreams Or Nightmares

The more I think about – and work with – dreams, the more amazed I am at the hidden workings of the human soul. We all dream, and the more attention we pay to our dreams, the more we become able to remember what we dreamed. Some people dream in black and white, others in colour; some remember smells and sounds, others mainly images. We might say: "I had this really strange dream last night. I wonder what that was all about... Oh well, probably just gobbledygook, just a load of rubbish..."

We don't understand the language of dreams; we never learned it. But imagine this: What if dreams *did* mean something? What if our unconscious were trying to tell us something, warn us about the way we live our lives, show us what's important right now and needs our attention? What if our souls were trying to offer us guidance and wisdom; what if there was a treasure buried within, and all we needed to do was to start listening, pay attention and make the effort to learn this "foreign" language?

Some people have the same dream time and time again, sometimes over many years. The unconscious is pointing something out to the dreamer and will persist, repeating the message over and over again until, maybe one day, the dreamer will understand... Of course we don't really know what "the soul" is. Some call it the unconscious, others may call it Guardian Angel, others might even experience this invisible part of ourselves as the connection to the Divine.

We all are looking for answers in one way or another; and usually we're looking on the outside. We don't know that the right answers for us can be found inside of ourselves, that there is a part of us that is much bigger, much wiser than our ego, our everyday awareness or conscious self. This Inner Wisdom can be accessed and consulted by each and every one of us. We may need a bit of help to learn this new language and to unearth this buried treasure that lies within ourselves.

It is the *real* treasure, unimaginably precious, awe inspiring and sacred. It is treasure that can't be stolen, lost or destroyed. It's were we find real answers, true guidance, the only real safety there is. Jesus Christ supposedly said: "The Kingdom of Heaven lies *within* you." Hinduism talks about "Maya"; that our perception of the world is an illusion. True freedom can only be found within ourselves.

Many more wise men and women said similar things, but we don't believe them; "we don't have ears to hear; we don't have eyes to see". – If you are still reading, you know by now how convinced I am of the importance dreams, of using them as a pathway to our own personal truth.

When we attempt to interpret dreams, it's important that we don't generalise. What matters in the interpretation is, to find out what the dream symbols mean to the *dreamer*; what their *personal* associations are; what clicks or resonates with them. We can feel it in our body when a certain interpretation hits the nail on the head; we will feel an actual "click": "Yes! This is it! This makes sense!"

Therapy can support and guide you on this rewarding journey towards the Centre of your Self. However, not all therapists work with dreams. If you're interested, you will have to find one that does.

29

Living Water

Water is a symbol for emotion and for the unconscious, our psyche or soul. We're now becoming much more aware of how important it is to live healthier, to eat good, natural foods, and generally taking better care of ourselves. However, we're not very good at taking care of our mental and emotional well-being; we don't learn very much at home and in school about how to deal with difficult or painful emotions, or how to form good relationships with ourselves and others.

We are all slowly (too slowly maybe) becoming more aware of the severity of the pollution of our planet, and of our oceans in particular. What we do to our planet is what we also do to ourselves. We push uncomfortable experiences or feelings away; we repress them, push them away into the unconscious where they pollute the psyche in the same way we pollute our earth, the living water of our oceans, our air: out of sight, out of mind.

The problem is that whatever we throw away, bury in the earth or chuck into the oceans, does not disappear. There is no "away". It's still there, accumulates and becomes toxic, destructive, and kills its inhabitants. We are poisoning the foundations of life, on our planet *and* in our psyche. "Rubbish" doesn't just disappear; we need to deal with it in a much more responsible, mature and constructive way, whether it concerns the material world or the inner world of the psyche or soul.

I'm aware that this sounds quite heavy, and we don't like heavy, we like lightness, fun, laughing things off. The problem is that, if we don't realise the destructiveness of our wasteful way of life and our love for ignorance, we might keep partying, and in blissful ignorance dance into the abyss…

INNER BALANCE

"If you do not change direction, you may end
up where you are heading."
Gautama Buddha

30

A Walk On The Wild Side

In Switzerland, where I grew up, February is the time when *"Fasnacht"* (Carnival), takes place. It is the time before Lent (fasting) begins, traditionally 40 days before Easter. This time of year always feels to me a bit like an in-between-land, still winter, but the end of it nearly in sight; still cold, but not so dark any more. But for three days and nights people are officially allowed to make *Fasnacht*, to "let the pig out", as the Swiss say; to go crazy and be wild and – very important – to make a lot of noise in order to drive out the bad spirits of winter and celebrate the coming of spring.

One very important aspect of *Fasnacht* is to tell the truth while wearing a mask. Some work for many months on these most elaborate objects. Some masks are huge and heavy; nearly all of them are outrageous and cheeky. Hidden by their masks, people make fun of everyone and everything. It's like soul-hygiene: What had to be swallowed and bottled up throughout the year can now be aired, by naming and shaming politicians, bankers and other culprits, without the danger of repercussions. In Basel people write long satirical poems that are then recited or sung in front of big audiences. In (Catholic) Lucerne, *Fasnacht* is outright archaic and anarchic. All hell breaks loose, as if all the devils and witches were having a big wild party. Imagine tens of thousands, or even a hundred thousand people "letting the pig out"!

I think it was (and is) very clever of Church and State to allow this wild time once a year. They let the people be unruly and naughty before it all gets serious and orderly again. There is an amazing, exciting energy; whole cities are vibrating and buzzing and boiling with all that unleashed energy that had to be held back all year long. It grabs you by the stomach and is incredibly exciting and invigorating! It's like being in a witch's cauldron and leaving all restraints of civilisation behind.

I think we are often "over-civilised" and over-controlled/over-controlling and repress our wild side, our shadow. We are trying to be in control of everything, and there is not enough space for the dynamic, creative parts of us. We are scared of them; they look like chaos to us, and we try anything and everything, to tame and repress these impulses. But nevertheless, they are part of us, of our psyche, and want to be acknowledged and expressed. They are an incredible life-force and could be the source of great creativity. If we don't acknowledge them, they will become twisted and destructive, and they *will* still find a way to manifest themselves. They will show up as anxiety, depression, anger, physical illness, or in differently destructive ways like crime, alcohol abuse that leads to violence and vandalism, and other nastiness. The fear of this life-force will show up as racism, nationalism, misogyny, fanaticism of any kind, which are all variations of the fear of the wild life-energy, and we attempt to alleviate these fears through control and division (in a nutshell). The thin veneer of civilisation disappears, and the shadow raises its head. On a national, extreme level, at the "right" moment under the "right" circumstances, the fear of these repressed energies can manifest itself in the form of a Nazi dictatorship or a Pol Pot/Khmer Rouge regime; in the form of any kind of terrorism, with no regard for humanity whatsoever. They are extreme attempts to gain absolute control. The more we fear and repress these energies, the more inhumane we become. So let's loosen up a bit, let's be more *aware* of our wild side and make more space for it. Let's be a bit less uptight, strict and over-controlling; let's go with the flow a bit more. Let's celebrate colourful diversity and variety! Let others live, and let *us live* a little more!

31

Destiny

Once upon a time there were a girl and a boy, and they were friends. They liked talking to each other, about all kinds of things. Sometimes their thinking went along similar lines, but just as often they had quite different viewpoints.

One day they had a debate about destiny and whether this idea should be taken seriously or not, whether our lives were pre-destined, planned and "written out" before we are born or, at the latest, at birth. The girl thought that this was rubbish and impossible; the boy wasn't so sure. "Who would make such a plan? Who or what would decide how people would live their lives and what would happen to them?" said the girl. "I don't believe in God anyway, and certainly not in that kind of God!" she added heatedly.

"I don't know what I believe," said the boy. "There are a lot of things that don't make sense if there is no God. But the old man who sits on a cloud makes no sense either..." And so it went on and on, and in the end they decided to go and see a neighbour, a middle-aged woman, who spent her days painting abstract paintings and was quite successful as an artist. They liked to talk to her because she always took them seriously and never talked down to them.

They found her in the garden, told her about their conundrum, and asked her what she thought of it. The woman smiled. "You don't mess about with the easy questions, do you?" she said. She was quiet for a while. "Well," she then said, "take an acorn for example. The plan for the oak tree is already there in the acorn. Whatever grows from the acorn *will* have to be an oak tree. It's its destiny to be an oak tree. If the young tree would decide to be, say, a conifer instead, maybe because it got the impression that conifers are better than oaks, it would get into serious trouble. It would never feel right; it might feel anxious or depressed or angry, and all because it tried to be something else than what it is *destined* to be by its innate nature."

"Wow," the boy called out excitedly, "so destiny is about being true to our nature, and that we get into trouble if we don't? Is that what you're saying?"

"That's right," said the woman, "at least that's how I see it."

The girl was deep in thought. "I think I know exactly what you mean," she said eventually. "Sometimes I feel that I'm not good enough the way I am and then I'm trying to be different, but it doesn't feel good."

"No," said the woman, "it doesn't feel good, does it…?"

(Acorn Theory: Plato, The Kabbalah, James Hillman)

32

Logos And Eros

I was going to sit down quietly and do some writing today. Then the phone rang (not for me), then the doorbell rang – a delivery (not for me either). Unfortunately, I then opened the post and discovered some quite complicated forms I need to complete. I started to feel anxious, overwhelmed. Several emails and text messages arrived, that demanded to be dealt with. All this happened within half an hour. Feeling positively beleaguered now, a slight panic began to rise: "Oh my goodness! Where do I start? I need to fill in these forms! I need to respond to all these messages! And what about my writing?!"

That's when I decided to stop and take a break. I left my office and made myself a sandwich and a cup of coffee. I sat down in the living room, put my feet up, took some deep breaths. Inwardly I said to myself: "You don't have to handle all this right now; there is time. Eat, drink your coffee, relax. Nothing bad is going to happen! Some people will have to wait a little. That's okay." Slowly I unruffled myself and calmed down.

Isn't this kind of scenario the norm for so many of us? – There is an endless stream of STUFF we need to deal with, endless demands and tasks, endlessly beeping and ringing phones, and we always feel behind, and live in constant stress and anxiety. Or we harden ourselves, shut down and power through it all. Logos takes over and runs the show. Logos: thinking, working, being logical and rational, structured and ordered, making lists and plans, trying to be in control. If its counterpart, Eros, has its place in our lives too, then that's okay; we need to make our lives work. But if Eros is out the window and forgotten, then the usual suspects turn up: anxiety, depression, panic attacks, anger, fear, stress.

Eros: fun, play, free time to ourselves, lighting a candle in the evening when the days are getting shorter again; a walk in the cool air, admiring the trees' autumnal display of colour; warming your hands on a hot cup of tea... Eros has to do with the senses, it's about reconnecting with ourselves, here, now, and with what's around us, seeing beauty, smelling or tasting something delicious, touching something comforting – like stroking the cat, listening to music that makes us feel good.

We live in a Logos-dominated world; work, chores, duties take over if we let them; drivenness is now seen as a virtue while our souls starve. The more starved we are of Eros, the worse we feel. Logos and Eros – we need them both, and they need to be balanced. If they aren't, then WE are out of balance, and we fall. The neglected parts of us will cry out, until we listen and restore the balance. When we are in balance, we are stable, and life feels good.

Therapy can help you to bring balance back into your life. Logos and Eros affect each and every aspect of our lives. Good therapy can support you in finding out how to take better care of yourself, and how to achieve an inner equilibrium.

33

Bring Back The Feminine

A while ago when on holiday in Malaga, Spain, I visited a basilica dedicated to the Virgin Mary. The magnificent church contained many statues of the Virgin, some with child, some without. They were all of life size, and dressed in splendid and rich real garments of velvet and silk.

I slowly walked around in the church, and at the end came to a statue of Mary alone, dressed in an opulent white gown, tears streaming down her face. I was very moved by this depiction and found myself speaking to her: "I know, it's so painful. But we're working on it, we'll do our best to bring you back into this world." To me, she represented the Feminine that is outcast from our world, from our lives, torn apart and split into the idealised, asexual Virgin/Mother and the demonised, all-sexual Whore. It is treated with contempt. It is trampled, attacked and raped. It is feared and hated. As persons and as a culture we're out of balance; the Masculine is domineering, and the Feminine suffers, in men *and* in women, since we all contain both principles.

I'm not saying that the Feminine is better than the Masculine, they're both equally important, but they need to balance each other. The Masculine principle as an archetype is about left-brain characteristics like analysis, logic, rationality, linearity, quantity, order, structure, achievement, solutions, thinking in words, about the *Letter* of the Law. If unbalanced, it becomes toxic, tyrannical, rigid, destructive, inhumane. If balanced and connected with the Feminine principle, it will be employed in the service of our *quality of life* in all areas, instead of in the service of faceless power, oppression, exploitation, greed, the destruction of the environment no matter what the consequences are.

The Feminine principle as an archetype is about right-brain characteristics, relatedness, interconnectedness, feeling, creativity, quality, context, inspiration, intuition, spirituality, process, living with the senses, thinking in images, about the *Spirit* of the Law. It's in flux, always changing, oscillating, adapting to each specific situation. If unbalanced, it will show up as flaky, childish, full of ideas that will never be realised, airy-fairy, ungrounded, all beauty and no substance.

If a man has a good connection to his inner Feminine (also called The inner She, the Muse, Anima, Soul) he will be confident and comfortable with his masculinity, strong but warm; his decisions will come from reason, but will be inspired and informed by creativity, empathy and intuition. If his relationship to The Inner She is problematic, she will express herself "sideways" and underhand, in a twisted way, and the man will be secretly insecure, moody, sulky, or a bully; he will be emotionally underdeveloped, immature, and he may be prone to aggression or depression.

If the Masculine in a woman is too weak, she may appear volatile, "flaky", chaotic, over-emotional. If the negative Masculine in her is dominant, she will constantly feel under attack and undermined by an inner bully (toxic masculine), telling her that she's not good enough; or she will appear hard, perfectionist, over-achieving, even obsessive. If the positive, supportive Masculine and the Feminine are in balance, she will be strong and clear, and also gentle and warm. She will be creative in her thinking and connected to and informed by her emotions but not overwhelmed by them. And: She will get things done.

We can call these principles "Yin and Yang" or

"left-brain/right-brain characteristics" instead of "Masculine and Feminine". – To me this seems more abstract, less tangible, even if the principles are the same. I'm aware that this is precarious territory; these principles can easily be misunderstood. They don't exist in their pure form in real life; they are dispositions. We all are on a spectrum of masculinity and femininity. However, we all live constantly with positive and negative experiences of being male or female, and these experiences have a deep impact on us. As a culture we're still half asleep in relation to their effects on our lives, and our mental and emotional well-being.

If we're troubled and unhappy, we could have a look at these inner dispositions and see whether some recognition and balancing is needed. Good therapy can help with this, so that we can disentangle ourselves from what often feels like inner chaos that makes no sense. It can help women and men to feel more robust and resilient, more real and authentic, more grounded and confident, more connected, warm and empathetic, more able to express themselves, and to live a richer, more colourful and fulfilling life.

34

One Step At A Time

I'm sitting at my desk, an empty page on the computer screen, and I'm waiting for inspiration: What shall I write about today? I'm closing my eyes, let ideas float through my mind, but nothing catches my attention. – I think: I just start writing and see what happens.

I rarely know what I'm going to write about when I sit down at my desk. I trust completely that an idea will come to me that excites me. I just start writing, whatever I notice outside the window, or whatever goes through my mind in that moment. I go with the flow, and eventually I always end up writing about something that interests me and fascinates me; something that has energy. I know that I can always change it; I don't need to get it right straight away. So I just begin. I don't know where it will take me; one thought leads to another, one sentence to the next.

This process is a bit like life itself. It's impossible to plan a whole life, or even the next five years, and then just follow a straight line to the set goal, although many people are trying to do exactly that. When we should choose an occupation (often in teenage years) or make a career plan, we often make this choice as "rationally" as possible: What's the job market like? Will my choice impress others? Will I get a good pension at the end of it?

We want to know the outcome before we even start. We want to be safe. Off we go, and all might go well and to plan. Then we get to the age of forty or fifty, and things begin to get sticky. We are bored out our minds, or our marriage or relationship falls apart. Maybe we spent the last twenty or thirty years paying a lot of attention to the packaging of our lives, but we didn't look after the content. I know of many marriages that look heavenly from the outside but are pure hell on the inside. I know of many people with a high income, with impressive jobs and titles, but who feel empty and depressed.

The Soul doesn't work in a straight line. If we listen to our Souls (our "Hearts") we only know the next step. The direction of the subsequent steps will depend on what we experienced so far. If we are trusting enough to live our lives in this way, we will often not know what will happen next, and where life will take us. This way of living may not seem very easy or safe, but it's full of LIFE. Of course it's great to have a good job or career, but it's the *content* that will keep us mentally and emotionally well and happy, not the packaging. It's the *warmth* in a family, that nourishes the Soul, not appearances. If you're unhappy with your life, it might be time to leave the trampled path and try something new. So – if you listen to your Soul – what are you hungry for; what are you longing for; what is *your* next step going to be?

35

Thinking With The Heart

Some Native Americans were very surprised when they learned that "the White Man" thinks with his head, because their experience was, that one thinks with one's heart. Chief Mountain Lake said to Carl Jung, when he visited the Pueblos, something like this: "We don't understand the white people; they're always looking for something. You can see the craziness in their eyes. What *are* they looking for!?"

He was right, we're always looking for *something,* and many of us don't know what they're looking for. We live in a "rational" age, and are proud of it. Intellect is what counts; academia, detached objectivity. We have huge problems in our societies, and can't seem to find solutions. Maybe that's because we think with our heads, not our hearts. Even a lot of therapists are aiming to work on a rational level, not including the soul, the

Inner World. Our souls are parched, thirsting for attention and care, for space and time to express their creativity.

To express emotions is frowned upon; it seems out of control, and it doesn't fit neatly into a box. We're afraid of the Irrational, the world of feeling, sensation and instinct. We're scared of what lies hidden under the surface of our rational minds, and we have cut ourselves off from our hearts. Some religious people have even banned their God (whatever God may be, maybe the Force of Life within ourselves?) into laws, rules and commandments. They even try to fit their *God* into a neat square box.

We live in a cold, rational world of intellectualism, and the paradox is, that the more rational we try to be, the more absurd our actions and decisions become, because we can't see the whole picture. – What would it mean to think with the heart? – It would mean to include feeling in our thinking: If you make a decision that affects others, how would it *feel* to be on the receiving end, to be in their shoes? Can you remember how it feels to be a child or teenager, and to be bossed around by adults?

To think with the heart, means to connect emotionally with everyone and everything around us, and to *care*. If we only think in a factual way, our relationships won't work, and our hearts will dry up and crust over. We will become hard-hearted, towards others and ourselves. We will dismiss the little voice inside that asks: Are you really living a rich and full life? Or are you just all work, facts, duties, and no play? When did you last play, day-dream and let your imagination run wild?

We're always looking for *something,* but we will never know what we're *really* looking for, if we don't start to think with our hearts.

36

Ego

We mostly talk about the ego in a negative way: A person has a big ego; somebody is too big for their boots, too full of themselves. The ego is the part of us that consists of our conscious mind, our conscious thoughts, emotions, memories, beliefs and knowledge. In short: It's the conscious ME. It makes judgements, makes sense of this world, processes information, contains reason and common sense. It also contains our identity, our understanding of who we are and who we want to be in this world. So it's really important to develop a strong and healthy ego, so that we know who we are, and become able to be independent, go out into the world and build a good life.

If our ego is too weak, for example because we didn't get enough support, love, encouragement or appreciation, we will find life difficult, we won't have a good sense of who we are and what we want. We might feel inferior, wounded, angry or depressed, suffer from low self-esteem. We might constantly have to deal with inner conflict, guilt and self-doubt. It's especially important to help children and teenagers to develop a good, strong ego, by mirroring them in a positive way: "I think you're really good at this or that; I understand what you mean; that's a very interesting thought; you are a lovely child; you are intelligent and beautiful; I'm convinced that you can do this!" etc. If we beat them down time and again, they will not be able to develop a strong, healthy sense of self and identity. They won't be able to find their feet in this world, to maintain loving, warm relationships, or to stand up for themselves.

The ego can also cause problems if it is inflated, if we totally overestimate our abilities and our importance, if we think that we're better and "bigger" than others. An oversized ego lacks substance; it's like a balloon, full of air. An oversized ego often covers up deep insecurity and fear of inadequacy, and overcompensates by being grandiose and pretentious.

Only a robust and resilient ego can be a good partner to our inner self, from where creativity, intuition and spiritedness come. In later life we might find that our standing in the outer world is not what matters so much anymore, that we naturally start to turn inwards. Then we may feel, that to utter an opinion about everything, loses its importance; that status and image aren't enough anymore; that we become more interested in insight, self-knowledge, and wisdom. But if we never had an ego of the right size, if it always was too big or too small, life will be difficult, scary or empty. So don't be afraid of ego-strength, of an ego with substance, integrity and authenticity. Without it, we can't mature; we can't become strong, loving and content. Without it, we can't live a good life.

37

Don't Be Too Good!

Many of us feel that we should constantly improve ourselves and our lives. We may dream of purity, of perfection, and we start to eliminate all the things from our lives that we consider as being bad.

Once I overheard a woman say: "I'm now totally addiction-free, I even stopped drinking coffee and tea." I think she didn't realise that wanting to be totally addiction-free can be an addiction as well. So many people today seem to be obsessed with being healthy. Of course it's important to look after our health, but health is not only about nutritious food and exercise. It's at least as much about the way we think and feel, about our attitudes to life.

There is a lot of anxiety and fear in that chase for perfect health and eternal youth, and anxiety and fear are not good for our health – physical or emotional. Are we forgetting to live whilst preserving ourselves for the future? And when is that future? – Why are we so terrified of getting older, of dying? I think that the fear of death is strongest in people who are not living a full live. We are too scared to live, we are scared stiff. Every day we are bombarded with scary news: This makes us ill, that gives us cancer, doom and gloom everywhere.

We live in fear and get paralysed by it. We don't try new things, we don't take a risk, we don't enjoy ourselves, we don't trust our bodies and their self-healing powers. We may live a very "pure" and structured life and become more and more rigid, and we stagnate. We do not grow and develop as persons, we try to stop the river from flowing and catch all the water of life behind a dam, to save it for the future...

If we strive for perfection, in any area of life, we are bound to fail. That critical inner voice, that keeps telling us that we are not good enough, will never ever be satisfied, and can drive us into depression.

So, don't be too good, too pure and "clean". Cut yourself a little slack, allow yourself to live and enjoy life, and let others live and breathe. The middle ground is where vibrant, joyful, life is!

38

New Boots For The Soul

I'm meeting a lot of people who are going through major changes in their lives. There is the man in his forties who decided after years of agonising, to give up his high-powered job as the manager of a building company, and to become self-employed. There is the man in his late fifties who runs a very successful international company and finds himself on the brink of a mental breakdown. He feels that his soul is crying out for more freedom and more time for creativity. There is the woman who runs her own kinesiology practice and who is getting divorced. She decided to buy her husband's half of the house from him and to become "her own woman".

Mostly these changes seem to be about working too much and not having enough time for oneself and one's family, about too much pressure from outside or driving oneself too hard; about being independent and being in charge of one's own life. All these people say that they felt boxed in and that this box is becoming too small for them. They want to be themselves, stop living a lie, express who they really are instead of fulfilling expectations from outside all the time. All of them are middle aged, and it seems they are all becoming "too big for their boots".

Boots that are too small cause a lot of pain and sooner or later start to split around the edges. They cut into the flesh and cripple one's feet. They can be very glamorous and shiny to look at, but excruciatingly painful to wear.

The great psychologist and thinker C. G. Jung thought that a lot of middle-aged people become depressed because their spiritual lives are poor, because they are mostly focused on their "outside" lives and don't develop their creativity, their inner world.

A spiritual life doesn't necessarily include religion (but it can). It's about becoming who we really are and are meant to become; about liberating our authentic selves; about expressing our creativity and living in a way that isn't just survival or habit, but makes us feel *alive.* It's about fulfilling our potential as a person. It's about the soul's longing to be acknowledged and nurtured, and the realisation that material goods cannot fulfil this longing.

Did you ever notice a battle between your heart and your head? Your heart knows what it wants, what feels right, but your head is afraid, and finds a hundred reasons why it isn't possible. The "too small boots" stand for stunted growth, for a starving heart or soul, for un-lived life and waisted potential, for a culture that wants to bind us and keep us small.

So, if you are getting "too big for your boots", you need new and bigger boots! Do take a risk and change your life; do stick your head above the parapet! Stop hiding your light under a bushel and stop concealing your talents and capabilities. Allow yourself to grow and shine! It's what we all are here for!

39

Where Is Home?

While writing this, I'm just getting ready for a trip to Switzerland. I haven't seen my family for almost a year and I really miss them. I only began to realise this after I moved to Britain: When I go there and spend some time with my family and friends, a side of me shows up that seems to go underground when I'm back in Britain. Maybe it's because most of them knew me all my life, or at least for a big part of it. Maybe it's because when back there, I speak in my native tongue, which seems to touch deeper or different layers of my soul. Maybe it's because when I'm there, I know in a different way who I am.

It's a paradox: Only when we leave our usual environment, are we becoming aware of what it really means to us, and how it made us who we are. I've been living in Britain for 24 years now, and it has become home to me too. I'm living on the fence, in a way. When I go to Switzerland, I tell people here in England: I'm going home to see my family. When I'm there, I say to my family: I'm going home to England. And wherever I am, I eventually start to miss the other country, its people and its language. They are both part of me now; both their languages and cultures live inside me now, and are still making me who I am and who I'm becoming.

Sometimes there is a bitter-sweet feeling in me, a kind of nostalgia, and I ask myself: Where is my home? Where do I belong? – But mostly I don't feel any more that I don't belong anywhere. More and more I feel that I belong to both countries, and that home is *within me*. It's not an outside place; it's a state of mind, or maybe a state of soul. Every so often I'm getting itchy feet; I want to go somewhere different, so that, by experiencing a different culture, I can experience myself in a new way and maybe discover parts of me that were unknown to me until now. It renews and invigorates me, to place myself into a new environment now and then. It helps me to see clearer, myself, the way I live my life, and the place I usually live at.

It's a similar thing with therapy: If my life doesn't work in one way or another I need to step outside of myself, so to speak, and look at it from a different perspective. This is what the therapy situation is for. It helps us to look at ourselves and our situation in a different light, with the help of another person. It can help us to understand, what *really* happens with us and our lives, so that we can start to see what needs changing and how it can be changed.

ADDICTION

COMPULSION

OBSESSION

"Staying vulnerable is a risk we have to take if
we want to experience connection."

Brené Brown

40

A Bird In A Cage

As a therapist I also work with people who suffer from addictions, and I meet people from all walks of life who battle with this problem. Some people tell me the most horrendous life stories, full of alcohol and drug abuse, violence and poverty (material or emotional, or both). I often wonder how they survived so much suffering, and I have deep respect for them.

Many live in a constant nightmare, and not only they themselves, but generations of ancestors before them, and their children and grandchildren after them. They can't see that their lives could be different, that there could be kindness, gentleness or even tenderness in a person's life. They grew up in abusive families (rich or poor) or institutions, and many of them had hardly any experience of kindness, respect, or trust. Addiction is about the lack of real, deep connection, and many people who suffer from serious addictions, have never experienced real connection to themselves and others.

Finally they find their way to therapy and experience maybe for the first time a relationship with a person who does not judge them, who does not put them down, who doesn't shout at them but who *listens,* and understands why they are so angry or sad, so desperate, so empty, so tormented by cravings. They have extremely good reasons to feel that way, and I tell them so.

Maybe for the first time they feel respected, accepted, understood; a positive connection with another person. Maybe for the first time they feel that someone listens to them and doesn't tell them to shut up, or that they're stupid, worthless or bad. Some of them can't take it. They don't know what to make of kindness; they get scared and just don't turn up any more.

Others soak it up like dry sponges. They want to talk, tell their story, and learn how to break the vicious cycle, how to relate and communicate with others in better ways. Some are really good at this; they go home and try out their new understanding, and sometimes they are rewarded with almost instant results: They stop nagging and criticising their family members, they start to respect them and thank them for what they do for them, and unsurprisingly, their partners, children, and friends, are relieved and respond in a positive way. These clients suddenly understand a simple truth: what goes round comes round.

I think this is true for all of us, even if our lives are not that nightmarish. Many of us haven't learned to relate and connect in constructive ways; we battle and row, and we just can't figure out how to improve things. We behave like a bird that has lived in a cage for all its life. Then somebody comes and opens the door but the bird doesn't know about freedom, and it stays in the cage because this is what it is familiar with. The bird needs to learn about freedom, and that there is a whole world out there that it didn't know about. That's what good therapy is about: to show that the door of the cage is open, and to help the bird to explore this vast world of new possibilities. Life can be so much better! If you can find the courage to take that step out of the cage, you will discover that you can fly.

41

Addiction: The Great Destroyer

If you have an alcohol problem it might really help you to go to AA (Alcoholics Anonymous). I myself am not a member of AA; that's why I can say this. AA members don't advertise AA, they don't try to convince people to join their fellowship; they "attract by example". But they welcome everyone who turns up because they know that it's not just about stopping drinking or taking drugs (NA – Narcotics Anonymous); that community is needed to support a process of deep inner change.

Addiction is a symptom; there are underlying reasons why we get addicted to substances or destructive behaviours. These reasons need to be addressed. It's not enough, just to stop drinking; we need to turn our lives around. If you're convinced that you're not addicted and that you could reduce or stop your intake or behaviour, try it. If you can do it without too much trouble, good on you! If you discover that you can't do it, that you find excuses, explanations, justifications, then you have a problem: You're in denial (forgive me for being so blunt).

I asked a long standing AA member and old friend of mine to read this chapter and to tell me if I'm being too blunt. He said: "With addicts one has to be blunt. The addict's perception of the world has become twisted. If we're honest with ourselves, we have to admit, that we don't really want to get sober. It's the compulsion. If there is a loophole or a back door, the addict *will* find it!"

Part of addiction is that we will avoid facing up to it at any cost. To become able to admit that we do have a drink or drug problem is the first step to change and healing. The second step is to get help. There is really not much point in trying to do it on your own; the likelihood that you will succeed is very small.

Alcoholism; workaholism; drug, sex and food addiction; gambling etc. are relational problems. It's about the relationship to ourselves and our own emotions, and our relationships with other people: They will either be quite bad; or they have been, or will be, destroyed. Isolation, which often comes from shame, is part of the problem, not part of the solution. We can't get better in isolation. We need community, connection with others who have gone through what we're going through. 12-step programs provide community and a safe space to connect with others, and to get support and real understanding.

Alcohol, drugs and gambling are THE big destroyers of families and relationships. Do you know how you behave when you're drunk, or high, or in debt up to the gills? Are your children scared of you? Do you argue a lot with the people around you; do you lie to them? Do you blame others for your troubles? – If we can't stand our lives when sober or clean, then we need to *change* ourselves and our lives.

Some people say: I don't want to go to 12-step programs because they're religious. That's a misunderstanding. They talk about a Higher Power, a "Power greater than ourselves" which can be "the God *of your understanding*" if you're a believer, no matter of which religion, denomination or conviction; or it can be the group, the community you're joining.

For me, another manifestation of the Higher Power is the psyche, the soul, the Inner Self. It knows what we individually need, in order to have a life that works. If we can surrender to the wisdom of the psyche, it will support and sustain us. 12-step programs can show you how it's done, how you can turn your life around, and so can good therapy. The problem is that therapy doesn't work if we regularly drink too much or get high. But therapy works very well alongside 12-step programs once you've stopped drinking or drug-taking.

Basically I see addiction as a form of fire-fighting of the psyche. We can't just stop the addiction; that's why it is an addiction, a compulsive behaviour, and it needs to be replaced with something else, something constructive, before we can let go of it. Jung defined addiction as a spiritual problem: The compulsiveness of it points towards an emergency in the psyche, a crushed inner spirit. We use substances or certain behaviours either because we can't feel anything without them, or because we can't stop feeling horrible feelings without them, or because we only feel alive when we take or do them, or because we're so empty that we try to fill this horrible emptiness by using them (e.g. food). Underneath it all: It's usually an attempt to control unbearable pain, to control an inner volcano of rage and prevent it from blowing up; and rage always covers up pain, despair and desolation.

This all-consuming pain comes from trauma, and being denied from the start of our lives the expression of our true inner nature, which is traumatic in itself: We're not allowed to be who we are, we're not nurtured and protected in who we are and are meant to become. Our needs are dismissed or ignored; we're not being seen and heard. From the start we are being chiselled and shaped and twisted and moulded into what other people think we should be and become. Add abuse and neglect of whatever kind, and imagine the result!

The rejection or vilification and abuse of our true nature, of WHO WE ARE, is excruciatingly painful and enraging. In order to survive, we soon learn to split off and disown these "dangerous" feelings, and to self-medicate, in whichever way we can. The addiction is in a way the lid that keeps the volcano from blowing, and we can't just take that lid away. We need to "defuse" the pressurised volcano slowly and safely, help it to release its content (pain, rage, shame, despair) slowly, so it won't just blow up and destroy everything in its vicinity, including itself.

Pain, rage, shame and despair need to be validated, listened to, understood, witnessed by a community that understands, like a 12-step group, or by a good therapist that isn't afraid of deep pain and rage. That's how the person with the addiction learns to reconnect with other human beings, and with themselves, with who they really are, warts and all. With connection comes healing, meaning and purpose. The duck realises that it is a duck. It can stop trying to be a squirrel, and for the first time in its life it will feel accepted, loved and celebrated as who it really is. That's what we all want, desperately. Simple really, but not easy at all. It takes work to claim ourselves back. And we can't do it on our own; that would be reinforcing our isolation, which obviously defeats the object. It's really okay to go and get help!

42

OCD: Let's Go Deeper!

There is now a lot of talk about OCD (Obsessive Compulsive Disorder) in the media, and it seems that more people suffer from it then is generally known. OCD has to do with intense anxiety and a lack of self-confidence, and can manifest itself for example through intrusive "bad" or fearful thoughts – that something terrible might happen to the sufferers themselves or others – the compulsion to clean or tidy up all the time, or to wash themselves incessantly because of fear of contamination through germs, or the compulsion to perform rituals like checking a certain number of times that the cooker is switched off or the door is locked. Also hoarding is a manifestation of OCD, and they are all about the fear that, if certain things are not done in "the right way", there might be disastrous consequences. Basically, there is a deep feeling of anxiety and insecurity. OCD can be extremely debilitating; it can deeply affect a person's relationships, school, work and social life.

There are many causes for OCD, anything that causes deep inner insecurity like growing up with violence and unpredictability, or overprotectiveness, or neglect. Also bereavement for example can cause OCD in the form of intense fears of illness or death. Any serious trauma can be the cause. But: Attempts to control intrusive thoughts and fears often don't work, because the root of the problem is not addressed. Often it's not enough to try and change certain behaviours or ways of thinking; a deeper approach is needed to achieve lasting change.

I don't really believe that forcing yourself to do the things that scare you most (like not cleaning all the time, or not checking the door lock repeatedly, or allowing germs on your skin) will make a real difference in the long run if the deeper lying insecurity and anxiety are not addressed. If they are addressed, then OCD might just start to soften or even disappear, almost as a by-product of deeper work. It's as if a terrified little child lives inside an OCD sufferer, and if that child in there doesn't get the reassurance it needs, it might just give up one kind of obsessive or compulsive behaviour and replace it with a different one. This extremely anxious part of a person is looking for protection or some control, in order to avert disaster; hence the rituals.

But, real protection can't be found on the outside; this work needs to be done on the inside, so that anxiety and fear can start to be replaced with trust and confidence. This can happen quite quickly for some people; for others it might take a while.

Unfortunately there are a lot of therapies for OCD out there that don't address the underlying issues and mainly focus on the symptoms rather than the root causes. If you are interested in a deeper approach, make sure you find the right therapist for you.

If OCD seriously interferes with your life, get help! Life doesn't *need* to be this hard!

FAMILY
MARRIAGE
RELATIONSHIPS

"Where love rules, there is no will to power, and
where power predominates, love is lacking.
The one is the shadow of the other."

Carl Gustav Jung

43

Thanks, Mum!

One day a few years ago, my mother called me for a chat, as we do, about once or twice a month. This phone call came just after a new baby, a little girl, had arrived in the family, and everyone was ecstatic. We got talking about having babies, how to raise children and how to love them best.

My mother started to tell me about my childhood, and how difficult it all had been back then in the sixties. We were five children and I was the oldest. We grew up on a small farm in Switzerland. Times were hard for farmers, and we were struggling.

Suddenly she said: "I know that you didn't get the love and support you would have needed; all of you children... You always seemed to be so independent and self-sufficient, even as a small child. I thought you were okay, and that you didn't need much attention or affection. In a way, that was a relief, because there were the other children, all that hard work on the farm, all those worries about money. But now I know that I was wrong, and that you were lonely. We did our best then, but it wasn't good enough. This is my biggest regret. If I could go back, that's what I would change."

I was stunned. I swallowed hard, but after we'd ended the call, the tears of relief came and didn't stop for several days on and off.

It had been my birthday that month, and what my mother said to me was the best birthday present ever. That she was able to say sorry to me in these words touched me deeply and was hugely liberating. A big burden suddenly fell off my shoulders, and after that phone call I felt how something in me was starting to open up towards my mother in a new way, effortlessly, and how we were getting closer, just because she had been able to acknowledge how it really was, all those years ago. I had never asked her to, but here it suddenly was, out of the blue, a gift of gold: the truth.

The interesting thing is: I now seem to be more able to admit shortcomings and to say sorry to other people, because I now know in a new and deeper way, that to say sorry, to acknowledge the truth, is not a loss of face. On the contrary; it opens the door to closeness, trust, authenticity and love.

Thanks, Mum!

44

Keeping On Growing Up

To be part of a "tightly knit" family is a strongly held value in most cultures. This can have advantages; we feel that we are part of something, that we belong. We feel supported, and the family is our safety net. However, it can also have disadvantages: We might never grow up properly, always depending on the family to be there for us. We might do things in order to make family or parents proud of us, instead of finding out what's *right for us,* in our own way. We might forever be the child that needs the parents' approval.

Some children won't leave home until they get married themselves; some parents are clinging to their children because their lives would feel empty without them, whether the children are living with them or not. This could be unhealthy for the children; they might never develop into rounded responsible adults, and it could be unhealthy for the parents, because they might avoid their own necessary further development, their own endeavour for a full and rich older age that contains more than being part of their children's lives. Parents who cling to their children, often need to be needed; what they're doing for their children is not really for the children, it is for themselves.

Rarely parents say: "Go out into the world, my child, and explore. Find out who you are and what's right for you. Go and find your own way. We love you, and we're here for you if you need us, but your life is yours. Don't try to make us proud, we are that already; go and make *yourself* proud!"

This doesn't only apply to young people; we might be in our forties or fifties and still looking to our parents for approval. We might be very grown up, capable and successful, but when we are with our parents, we might immediately fall back into the child position, looking for their approval. This can be very debilitating and disempowering. It will undermine our self-confidence and self-worth. It will forever bind us, and distract us from finding our own way, our own solutions.

To free.ourselves from this tether might in some cases cause tension with parents and/or family, and we have to become strong enough to live with their disapproval, so that we can be ourselves and find appreciation within ourselves. They might try to pull us back into the fold in order to secure their influence on us. If that's the case, we need to cut the emotional umbilical cord, so that we can truly grow up and live our lives our own way. You can still love your parents/family/children *and* live your own life. You can keep loving them even if they disapprove of your way of life. To be true to yourself is more important than to please others.

45

Are You A "Character"?

Normally, if we say that somebody is a "Character", we mean that this person is a bit different from the rest of us, that they do things their own way, that they are unconventional. Most people find it quite scary to stick out from the masses and we try very hard to adapt and fulfil what we think is expected of us. I'm thinking for example of all the parents driving their teenagers around all day, from one appointment to the next. They feel that, if they wouldn't do this, they would be seen as bad parents, and we forget that it is healthy for children to learn to be independent and self-responsible.

Or children's birthday parties: Each one has to be grander than the last one, and there is now the expectation that each child at the party has to be given a present as well, which costs a lot and causes a lot of stress for parents; but everybody does it because they feel it's expected.

Or: How often are you going to parties where you stand around with a glass in your hand, small-talking your way through the evening, saying the same things and asking the same questions again and again while you are bored out of your mind and can't wait for the moment when you can leave without causing offence?

How often do you feel you have to pretend that you're living in a happy relationship, and that everything is fine with you and your family, because everybody else seems to be fine? You fear you would be seen as a failure if you admitted that things aren't so rosy after all. How many people even have children because it's what's expected and makes them feel like worthy members of society? We do whatever we can to be seen as "proper" people and we wouldn't for the world want to be seen as "characters". But: What is the price we pay in order to be "proper"? – I think the danger is that we betray ourselves, and that we lead a kind of double life. We hide what we really think and feel, and who we really are. We try to be what we think we should be, and we forget who we are on the inside. We teach our children that appearances are everything, and social media pressure adds to this destructive way of living. Many people never even have the chance to discover who they really are; what they think and want; how they want to live their lives. We sacrifice our true self and put a lot of effort into developing a mask, a false self: We tear ourselves apart.

This is the unrecognised cause for so much inner conflict, anxiety and depression, and also for physical illnesses that paralyse us. – Have you ever imagined how liberating it would be, to do things *your* way, to refuse to do what everybody else does? To have backbone, moral fibre, to *have* character? To be able to breathe freely and not to be scared of what others think? To let them have their opinions and to have your own, maybe different, convictions, and live accordingly? – What an exciting and colourful world we would live in if we could learn to be true to ourselves, to be free, to be Characters!

46

Being A Martyr

Christmas is approaching fast, and many people are beginning to feel stressed and apprehensive. Nearly everybody you meet will ask: "Are you ready for Christmas?" And most probably you will say: "No, not even close! I can't wait till it's all over!" – Isn't this a shame? There is a potentially lovely festival coming up, and we all dread it; mostly, I think, because we see it as being about doing the done thing and fulfilling other people's expectations.

But do we have to? Isn't this just one more occasion on which we dismiss our feelings of stress and anxiety instead of taking them as a sign that we – yet again – are about to ignore what we would *really* like to do? Why not make it simpler, nice and relaxing? Why not be creative and invent a new way of celebrating, one that everybody, including you, could enjoy? – Maybe you think that you have to follow the same procedure as every year, because your family and relatives expect you to, and you convince yourself that they will feel let down if you don't. But are you sure about that? Are you sure that *they* enjoy it? Or is it possibly as torturous for them as it is for you? Have you ever asked them, or suggested a different way of celebrating? Have you ever considered not travelling all over the country – or even beyond – to visit dozens of people? Why not spread these visits out a bit?

I think it's very probable that, if you find yourself in the role of a martyr at Christmas (doing what you think is expected of you and ignoring your own wishes but then feeling resentful), you do it all year round. This is about trying to protect other people's feelings (which is really a form of control) at your own expense. You may say: "But what if they are upset?" – I doubt that they would be but if they are, let them! It's their right to feel whatever they chose to feel, and it's not your responsibility to make them feel differently. It *is* your responsibility, however, to say what you are willing to do, and what not. Then you can start to negotiate and work out together what will be done, so that it's enjoyable for everybody.

Some compromising may be necessary, from all involved. But you will notice that the resentments will disappear as soon as you speak up and make your position clear. Maybe you will feel a little guilty for a moment or two – which is to be expected because you are breaking with a convention – but that's okay; you will survive, and the guilt will soon dissolve. Then you can get on with enjoying yourself because you are doing what you really want and like to do!

47

"Don't Be So Selfish!"

If you want to manipulate or guilt-trip somebody because they don't do what you want them to do, all you need to say to them is: "You're so selfish!" To call somebody selfish is the big hammer, it works with nearly everybody, and they will immediately feel guilty. We never really think it through. It's totally ingrained in us that to do what we want to do, to put ourselves first sometimes, is selfish. For hundreds of years selflessness was promoted, especially for women, in order to keep them in their place.

It's quite complicated. Of course there is selfishness. We are selfish if we have no consideration for others, if we are only concerned with our own benefit or pleasure, if we think the world revolves around us, that everything is about us and everybody else should be concerned with us. It's a deep, sometimes ruthless neediness that makes us blind for others and their needs and experiences. Some people can only talk about themselves, and if you tell them about yourself, they will immediately say that the same thing happened to them, but of course much worse! Truly selfish people are incapable of compassion or even of consideration of others. But if we would dig into the life story of such a person, it's highly likely that we would find unprocessed trauma, physical and/or emotional neglect and starvation, and other forms of abuse, in their past. They are still craving the undivided attention they never had, in a very unconscious way, and without taking responsibility for the fulfilment of their needs. The therapeutic challenge to them would be to learn how to give themselves the love and attention they are so desperately looking for in others.

It's often "selfish" people who will accuse others of being selfish, in order to manipulate them into submission. The word "selfish" is probably one of the most abused words in history. It's *not* selfish to have needs, to know what they are and to fulfil them. It's *not* selfish to do what feels right for you. It's *not* selfish to put yourself first now and then, and to treat yourself to some time on your own; to a corner or even a whole room (!) in your house, that is going to be *your* space from now on. It's *not* selfish to have other interests than family or work; something that is just for you and will make you feel good.

It's called Self-Care. To neglect ourselves and what we want and need, out of fear of being seen as selfish, is not a healthy thing to do. To force ourselves to live in a way that makes us feel bad, depressed, frustrated, even angry or resentful, is not helpful for our mental and emotional well-being. Basically it's about allowing yourself to be who you are and to give yourself what you need, even if some people might not like this, because they can't use you for their own purposes any more. – Then turn it around and check yourself: It's also about allowing others to be who they are, and to get for themselves what they need, even if you might not like this, because you can't use them for your own purposes any more. Allow them to be themselves and don't call them selfish. And do the same for yourself. Life is not about crushing ourselves and each other, it's about learning how to blossom!

48

Heroes

A while ago I saw a news report about the novelist Cara Hoffman's appeal to stop calling soldiers Heroes. I immediately paid attention, because for a long time now I've felt the same, and not only about soldiers. The word Hero comes from the Greek for Demi-God, and that, we are not. If we call somebody a Hero, we put them on a pedestal and don't allow them to be human anymore, with all the flaws and so-called weaknesses that all human beings have.

For example, if we tell someone who cares for a sick person, or suffers from an illness, or lost a loved one, or an overwhelmed mother or father, how strong and amazing they are, they usually feel that they have to live up to this image, that they *have* to be strong and amazing at all times. They feel they are not allowed to be exhausted, sad and fed up, let alone admit it to someone else, or even ask for help.

It becomes unacceptable, and they will feel that they themselves become unacceptable if they show what they really feel.

If we call soldiers Heroes, we deny them the possibility to speak of their suffering, of the horrors they saw and the fear they experienced, whether they lost limbs or not. If we call any person who lives in a difficult situation amazing, marvellous, admirable etc., we may rob them of the chance to express how they truly feel, and we potentially push them into isolation and loneliness. Many people around us run on fumes and constantly live on the verge of a breakdown, but still feel that they have to put on a brave face. They feel that they should be able to handle their situation better, and they feel guilt and shame about the fact that they can't really live up to the expectation to be strong and marvellous.

Maybe you are one of them? – If so, don't put up with it any more. Refuse the role of the Hero or Heroine, of the superman or superwoman. Give yourself permission to be honest and authentic, and to ask for help. If you know someone who is trapped in the role of the Hero, let them know that it's totally understandable if they feel fed up and desperate sometimes.

If we idealise people, we push them into

isolation. If we say: "I could never do what you do; I could never cope with what you cope with," we imply that they are stronger than we are. But they are not. We just make them feel that they should be. And if someone *does* show their true feelings, don't try to console them by pointing out the good things in their lives; don't try to make them feel better. If you show that you understand how they feel, they *will* feel a little better, just because you listened.

Of course there are people who do heroic things; I'm not denying that. But even then, they are not demi-gods; they're still human and need human empathy and compassion.

49

Relationships:

A Riddle, A Puzzle, A Mystery!

Of course I, too, watched the Royal Wedding of William and Kate in 2011, together with millions of others. I asked myself why I wanted to watch it, and one reason may be that, being Swiss, it gives me a sense of belonging to watch these utterly British kinds of events. I just loved the glamour and beauty of it!

In Switzerland we have no Royal Family, only seven ordinary people who form the government, and most of them go to work by train and bus. No glamour there! Another reason why millions watched this beautiful wedding might be that we all dream, openly or secretly, of this fairy tale, and of living happily ever after. But of course it is a fairy tale, and the real work only begins after the wedding.

Apparently, some people got quite upset while watching the Royal Wedding, because they mourned their own "failed" marriages, or they realised, battling with their own difficult relationships, that it *is* a fairy tale, and not reality. And yet, we still get fed this dream of romance and everlasting happiness by books and films and social media. We hope against hope, that this dream might come true for us; that *we* might be different, even if there is so much evidence of the contrary all around us. We seem to be immune to the known facts of divorce rates and relationship misery. The dream of the fairy tale seems to make us blind for reality.

I often wonder why we don't teach children life skills, like how relationships work, what it takes to make a relationship blossom and thrive. We don't teach them about why people argue and how they could stop arguing and make their lives happier. We still believe that marital happiness is about luck, a bit like the lottery. **So, why are we, as a culture, relationship-illiterates?** – Nearly all misery in our lives has to do with our inability to relate in constructive ways. We just don't know how to do it! It seems like a mystery, a riddle, a puzzle with missing pieces. If things get sticky, we think that it's the other person's fault; and if they would change, we could be happy. It could be the spouse, the boss, our colleagues, the driver in the car in front of us, our parents or children. If they were different, all would be well. But they are not different, and probably never will be.

We don't understand that we can't change other people; that I can only change *myself* – and that only *I* can change myself. And: If I change and make myself happier, the dynamics in my relationships will change, because *I* am different. By believing that *they* should change, we turn ourselves into powerless, helpless victims. But by realising that the only person I can change is *ME*, I can get the power over my life back. I know, easier said than done. But that's where therapy comes in: It's one possible way of learning about ourselves, and how to improve our lives; about learning to take responsibility for our happiness instead of blaming others for our misery. So, take your happiness into your own hands. Power to YOU!

50

Happily Ever After...

Are you happy in your marriage or relationship? Have you found your prince or princess, and does your partner fulfil your expectations? Does he or she take care of your every need? – Or are you disappointed in your partner? Do you think if he or she would change, you would be happier? Do you even feel that it's his or her job to fulfil your needs, and that your happiness lies in their hands? Maybe you feel trapped, powerless and frustrated, even hostile about the shortcomings of your prince or princess who turned out to be more frog than royalty. Now what? – Put up with it? Or find somebody new and better? – But what if that new somebody turns out to be as human and inadequate as your old model?

I think we are all on the wrong track with our ideas and dreams about relationships and happiness. We want our partner to be our mother, our father, not the ones we had, but the ones we always wanted and would have needed. Like children, we are looking to them to look after us, to make us feel safe and happy. But we are not children anymore; we are grown-ups, at least on the outside. Our partners can't make us happy; it's not their job, it's *our* job. Only *I* can look after myself in the way I need it; my happiness lies in *my* hands and nobody else's. *I* am responsible for my needs and their fulfilment, nobody else is.

My partner is my mirror, my teacher. What I don't like in them, is what I reject in myself, or *what I don't allow myself to be*. What I hate in them, is what I don't want to look at in myself. I have the perfect partner, exactly the one I need, in order to learn what I need to learn, so that I can emotionally grow up, and be responsible for myself. What we can't recognise in ourselves, we project outside ourselves onto others, so that we can *see* it out there. The error is, that we think we can change it out there. That never works. We can only change it inside ourselves. Then we are in charge again, in charge of ourselves and our lives. Then we own our personal power, and we are not helpless any more. Then our relationships will improve in miraculous ways; or our paths will part, not out of helpless hatred, but because this is not where we're supposed to be any more, after we've changed.

There is a wonderful book that explains all this in much more depth. It's the best book I've ever read about relationships: It's called *Love yourself, and it doesn't matter who you marry*, by the German psychotherapist Eva-Maria Zurhorst. A provocative title, but oh so true. If I learn what it means to love myself I will improve my relationship no end, or I will pick someone who loves him- or herself too. *Then* we can truly connect and relate to each other!

51

Drama Queen, Drama King

There are dramas played out in nearly every family or relationship. Some are loud and dramatic, some are silent. When I speak of drama, I mean a specific way of relating – or better: not-relating – to each other. We all bicker sometimes, and a good argument now and then clears the air; there is nothing wrong with that. It becomes difficult though, if we are so full of resentments, that we are unable to relate to others in an open, direct, and constructive way.

The Drama Triangle dynamic is destructive; it doesn't go anywhere; we go round and round in circles. We play mind games; we try to manipulate; we play the blame-game; we try to make the other person feel guilty, or tell them, that, if they would behave differently, all would be better. In short: We don't want to take responsibility for our part in the problem, or our feelings; we want the other person to be responsible for our misery. Here is a diagram that illustrates this destructive dynamic:

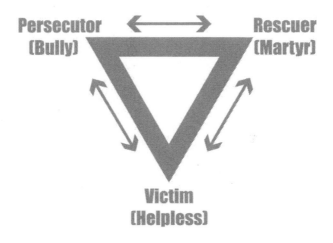

(Diagram by Stephen Karpman M.D.)

- If we are in the position of the **Persecutor** (bullying, intimidating) we attack the other person, criticise them, try to control them. We try to force them to be the way we want them to be. We might even use violence.

- In the **Victim position** we feel hard done by, hurt, treated unfairly, helpless. We blame the other person for the way they are, do, or say things. We don't take responsibility for our needs; we say: *You need to change, to make me feel better.*

- If we are a **Rescuer**, we always try to solve

other people's problems; we think we know better; that without our intervention things will go wrong; and that we are more capable than others to do things "the right way". But then feel resentful for "having to do everything and not getting any gratitude".

Of course we don't stay in one position all the time; we move from one corner of the triangle to another. If a Rescuer is rebuffed, they then turn into a Victim: "I only wanted to help", they might say, and walk away sulking, or they turn into a Persecutor and attack the rebuffer: "But you never do things right, you're useless!" they might shout. Persecutors may feel that *they* are the Victim while they attack others. Victims may turn around and have a go at who they feel attacked by, or even attack the Rescuer, and turn into the Persecutor.

You can see that this dynamic has many facets, but whenever we attack and blame one another, we're trapped in it. This may be done by sniping, needling or shouting, or it may happen in silence: We are secretly angry or contemptuous, but we never say anything, and our relationships turn silent, distant, and hostile, when all the unspoken stuff builds up like a mountain between us.

This game can be played by one person, in their own mind; by any kind of pair; by whole families, or even by a whole nation. Here we usually call it "politics". Nations also play this game with each other. One of many ways they play it, is called "war".

But: There is hope! We can free ourselves from this endless vicious triangle by taking responsibility. Which means: For example, as a couple, we stop saying "YOU always do this; YOU never do that," etc. Instead we could learn to talk about ourselves and say: "I feel lonely, cut off from you. I feel resentful or angry. I feel taken for granted. I need your help. I need a hug. I am grumpy today. I am sorry." And we leave it at that. If the other person responds with anger, we don't start to argue. We might go and do something else for a while, and give them some space until everyone has calmed down and we can talk it through and listen to each other properly.

The pull of the Drama Triangle is extremely strong, like a compulsion. It's hard to stay away from it; and staying in it might even give us a bitter kind of satisfaction. But if you persist, your relationships will improve! Therapy can support you in this liberating endeavour.

52

Falling In And Out Of Love

Falling in Love is one of life's great mysteries. We all carry an image in our souls: that of the God or Goddess of Love. One day, we meet a person who seems to be the incarnation of that God or Goddess; the world turns upside down, and we fall into the sky. Something seems to take possession of us that we can't control. We worship this god-like person, we only see the good in them, we see what we want to see, and if there is a little voice of reason left within us, we silence it. This person fulfils our dreams of being recognised, cherished and loved. All is perfect; he or she must be the One, the One we were waiting, hoping, praying for. We live on a fluffy cloud of romance, and everything looks rosy.

And then one day, this perfect lover will say or do something that causes a jolt in our stomach, something that feels hurtful, something that touches a raw nerve within us, and we are confused: What's happening? How can this perfect person say or do something like this? – This may happen a few times, and we may be able to push it to the side for a while, but in the end the fluffy cloud dissolves, and we land on the ground with a bump. We finally realise that our God or Goddess of Love is an ordinary human being, a normal person (like we are ourselves), and disappointment sets in. We feel deceived, cheated of our dream of having found the One who will shoulder the burden of our fulfilment; the One who will dedicate his or her life to our happiness.

But, we are not ready to give up just yet; we start arguing, criticising, bickering, splitting hairs. We demand that our lover develops the super-human qualities we wanted to *believe* they had; we demand that they change for our sake. We refuse to accept that they are human, not god-like, and we refuse to accept them as they are, with all the good, the irritating and the imperfect.

Some couples get through these bumpy times; they begin to realise that romance is not love, and over time they become able to respect and appreciate each other as they are. That's when true, human love slowly starts to grow. That's when the world rights itself, when we take off the rose-tinted glasses and become willing to see things as they really are. This kind of love is much more down to earth, much less dramatic, and full of a quiet kind of tenderness, even if our lover is irritating at times.

It also means, that we become willing and able to take back that projection of godliness with which we previously burdened our partner, and we agree to grow up a bit more, to be responsible for our needs and their fulfilment, instead of putting that responsibility into our lover's hands. To take responsibility for myself means: to *respond to myself*, my deeds, my needs. *This* is how we will begin to experience ourselves as being whole, complete. No-one else can make us complete.

And yet, the process of falling in love is a beautiful and necessary one. It's how we get together with another person in the first place. Without it, we might never even bother. And it is this sometimes painful process of persevering on this journey from romantic, seemingly divine love, to the more mundane and down-to earth, human kind of love, that will make us grow, grow up, and mature into a person with true inner substance. If we survive this bumpy ride, we will live in truly successful relationships, with our lover, and with ourselves.

53

Small Talk

Therapists often chose their profession because they themselves benefited so much from therapy, and they want to offer this opportunity to others as well: the opportunity to be in real connection with another human being by talking about the things that we normally don't talk about, the things that really matter in a person's life.

There is a lot to be said for small talk; it helps us to gently get to know someone. It's really useful for first contact and to find out whether we feel comfortable with someone. It's also an important part of family life and of all kinds of relationships as a repeated bonding exercise. Some animals bond by grooming each other and picking parasites out of each other's coats; humans use small talk for that same purpose. Only, it can become a problem if that's the only way we talk to and connect with others, especially in relationships that are meant to be close.

If a couple ends up only small-talking to each other, it's extremely likely that things are not going very well in their relationship. If parents and children only talk about practical, "educational" or organisational things, then their connection won't be as deep as it could be and needs to be, in order to enable emotional well-being. Personal, intimate, conversations are absolutely crucial in building a deep and strong connection with someone else. By personal conversation I mean telling someone how we *really* feel, good or bad, being honest about things that excite or trouble us, sharing the things that really interest or confuse us. If we end up only small-talking to the partner, parent or child, we are at the same time hiding a huge amount of ourselves. We *hide* what we really think, what's important to us, who we truly are. If we do that, then we can't truly connect with others. Hiding our true feelings and thoughts will make us lonely, can even cause depression, and will create a wall between ourselves and others; and every time we small-talk instead, we add another stone to the wall until it feels insurmountable.

Personal conversation also includes genuinely felt words of love and warmth, of appreciation and gratitude, of understanding and showing interest.

And: It includes a great deal of *listening without judging.* Try this with your stroppy teenager, and small miracles might yet happen.

Very slowly we begin to realise, that emotional health is as important as physical health. The mind is not a machine, nor is the body. Pills and techniques alone will not enable emotional health. The foundation of good emotional health is real, deep, loving connection – the knowledge that I'm held in someone else's love, and that I hold them in my love.

54

It Takes Two To Tango

Relationships can bring a lot of joy and fulfilment if we know how to look after them. This may sound strange, but unfortunately most of us never learn anywhere, not at home and not in school, how to make relationships work. For many couples, their relationship is the most demanding and confusing thing they ever deal with in their lives. If you and your partner just happily sail along with no major conflicts, you're either very lucky or you bottle up a lot of scary feelings, like anger, disappointment, resentment, sadness or loneliness.

For most couples, it's not plain sailing, even if it looks like that from the outside. Being in a long-term relationship can be very challenging indeed. Some people feel that their partner is not listening, isn't willing to talk about feelings, or anything much at all, and that they use the relationship like a petrol station where they refuel and recharge but don't really engage with their partners. They see their partner more like a parent replacement (food on the table, laundry done, wood chopped, money in the bank etc.) and they can't see why they should grow up, give back and contribute, and look after their partner as well.

Others feel that their partner is too demanding, always nagging, always wanting to talk, and not giving them any peace. A lot of people feel, that if their partner would change in certain ways, all would be well. They are convinced that it's all the other's fault, whatever the problems between them are. But of course that's only half the story. It takes two to tango, and it takes two who are willing to turn things around. We often go into a relationship with the hope that the other person will make us happy and fulfil our needs. This is partly right, but only partly. We have to be willing to give back as much as we get. We all have a history, and bring baggage into a relationship; and we may be living under the illusion that our partner should give us what we never had. Normally, this is too much to ask, and partners can feel overwhelmed by these demands.

There are also partners who don't know how to listen properly, or how to speak out and say what they feel and think, and how to do this in a way that brings positive results. Some partners think that the relationship is fine, while the other one feels neglected and lonely. Learning how to communicate is paramount! It's the foundation on which good relationships can be built. If your attempts at communicating always turn into rows, then you are caught up in a "drama-dynamic". In couple-therapy you can work on how to step out of this destructive dynamic, and how to talk things through in a way that will make both partners feel heard and appreciated. A relationship will get better, if both partners are willing to do this work, which consists of truly listening, of being honest and authentic, of taking responsibility for our part of the difficulties, and of stopping the blame game. No blaming! No more "YOU always do this; YOU never do that." Instead, we need to learn to talk about ourselves: "I feel lonely. I feel sad. I feel angry." And, we need to learn to really, deeply, listen.

Relationships are like gardens. Being in a relationship is like learning to look after a garden together. If we both put a good amount of work and care into it, it will blossom and thrive. If we neglect it, it will wither and die, or turn into a wilderness and suffocate. Don't you think it's worth the effort?

55

"It's All Your Fault!"

To stop blaming others for the difficulties in our lives, is one of the trickiest challenges we will ever encounter. It is so hard! The compulsion to blame, to think that it's all someone else's fault, is almost as strong as the gravitational pull of a black hole, one of those mysterious invisible phenomena in outer space, that pull everything in their vicinity into themselves, and swallow even light. We are absolutely, totally, one hundred percent convinced, that, whatever the problem is, it's not our fault; it's the other persons fault, and that *they* have to change, so that *we* can feel better.

Even the idea that I might have my part in it, might seem preposterous. But: To sit down with myself and seriously consider this possibility, even if every part of my being protests against it, is the only way forward. To insist that "it's all your fault", makes us feel powerless, and turns us into seemingly helpless victims. By demanding that YOU change, I might bang my head endlessly against a brick wall, but it won't get me anywhere. Blaming others can give us a strange sense of bitter satisfaction, the satisfaction of our own righteousness: I'm helpless here, but I'm righteous, and I'm right! Somebody once said: "Be right, or be happy." To let go of the conviction that I'm right, is as painful as stopping to blame others.

"Being right" doesn't get us anywhere in any relationship. It's not about blaming *ourselves* instead of others; blame is a totally useless and destructive concept in any scenario. It's more about examining myself and the situation I'm in, and to be willing to understand, how this situation developed, and what my contribution to it was or is. It means, that I take the power over my life and the responsibility for myself back into my own hands. This *will* be a painful process, and we might even be confused for a while. We may need to grow up quite a bit, and learn to bear the confusion until clarity emerges.

To bear an uncomfortable situation for a while, is what we all try to avoid. It takes strong emotional muscles to resist the mighty pull of the Black Hole of Blame, and to bear the unpleasant realisation, that I have helped to create the situation I find myself in.

One day, while we had an argument, my husband paused, then said to me calmly, and *not* in a manipulative, attacking way as most of us so often do: "You are quite defensive right now, aren't you?"

I just caught myself, and stopped, before I was going to defensively shout at him: "No, I'm not!" Instead I just about managed to say: "Yes, I am, aren't I!"

We both burst out laughing, and the argument was over. Usually, the defensive impulses are quicker than the rational mind, and we hit back before we think; we get sucked into the Black Hole of Drama before we even realise it. This time I managed to my own surprise, not to fall (or jump) into the hole, and I was deeply astonished, how liberating it was! I didn't need to fight any more; I somehow managed to admit an uncomfortable truth about myself, and the fight just dissipated.

The way forward is to allow for the possibility that I might have a part in our difficulties, to ponder it and live with it for a while, even if I don't understand yet what my contribution to the problem is or was. It feels like turning all our beliefs and convictions on the head; but what we really do, is to turn *ourselves* back on our feet.

Dispassionate self-examination is a very demanding thing to do indeed, but only self-knowledge brings real freedom.

56

Marriage

Marriage is not what we think it is. In our culture we have the collective understanding that marriage should be a happy union of two people, and we think that, if it isn't mainly happy and problem-free, we are failing, or are doing something wrong. Romantic stories usually have a happy ending; two people finally get their act together, and are getting married. The expectation is that they will now live happily ever after. But of course they usually don't.

On a social level, marriage is often seen as being about reproduction, and about upholding traditional structures and values of society. On a psychological level, however, marriage is about something completely different: It's about friction. After a honeymoon period, friction will set in, and this is exactly what's supposed to happen. This may sound baffling, or even absurd, and it goes totally against our expectations and beliefs. We think that when we get married, everything should fall into place, but in reality it's the contrary: All the puzzle pieces are thrown in the air, and so the adventure begins. Marriage is here to challenge us, to bring forth all the issues we buried, to press all our buttons, to trigger in us the whole of our repressed life history that we hoped to leave behind us *by* getting married.

Marriage figures among the greatest challenges life may present us with, and it is also one of the greatest opportunities to grow and develop as persons. If our marriage "doesn't work", we usually like to think that, if our partner would change, all would be well. But again: The contrary is the case. It's me that needs to change, it's me I need to look at, it's me I need to work on, and this applies to *both partners*; this is about stopping the blame game and starting to take responsibility for *my* part of the problem. Even if my part is, that I'm staying in an abusive relationship, and that the challenge for me is to find a way to leave. Abuse and violence are unacceptable.

However, I'm also talking about everyday irritation or disappointment, the disagreements and misunderstandings, the banal, silent dissatisfaction. It's almost as if we needed to learn to look at our marriages in an abstract way: This person is in my life and bugs me because he or she brings all my unresolved issues to the surface, and so gives me the opportunity to see and address them. For me, it was hugely liberating to realise and accept that it's okay to have disagreements, friction, arguments, that it's even okay to be unhappy for periods of time, and that this doesn't mean that the relationship isn't working. It was and is in those times, when things feel difficult, even painful, that I learn most about myself, my unrealistic expectations towards my partner, my wanting to be looked after instead of learning to look after myself, my narcissistic attitude of "me me me", my rejecting to imagine myself in my partner's shoes for once. Marriage is the School of Growing Up, and it really hurts at times.

On this level, it almost doesn't matter whom we marry; whoever it is, they *will* put the finger on our blind spots and trigger our old wounds, without even being aware of it, just by being there: low self-esteem; inner insecurity; repressed anger, trauma, pain, anxiety etc. Whatever it may be, we usually want our partner to make us feel better by being or not being a certain way, by doing or not doing certain things. It never works; they can't make us feel better, safer, happier. It's our responsibility to do this for ourselves. The challenge is, to realise this, and to work with it, preferably with the help of someone who can support us through this process of self-recognition and positive change, like a good therapist.

But there is more: Ultimately, it's about our *inner* union, our marriage with ourselves, the reunion of the parts of ourselves that we have split off, buried, rejected, repressed, and vehemently deny. Only then can we become complete; only then can we truly fulfil the purpose of our existence. In this sense, the outer marriage is a representation of an inner process. There is nothing more demanding and challenging we could ever undertake; and there is nothing more rewarding, liberating and fulfilling. In Jungian language it's called "The process of Individuation", of becoming an Individual, which means: an indivisible Whole.

57

All You Need To Do Is To Love...

Valentine's Day: With Christmas just behind us, there is already another event looming on the horizon that might be slightly tricky for some of us: Valentine's Day. – Maybe you are freshly in love and feeling all romantic. Maybe you are in a happy and stable relationship and the Valentine's routine is a positive one for you.

Or maybe you are not one of those lucky ones, you might feel that your relationship is a bit tired, not going anywhere or, even worse, you feel you are drifting apart and the whole thing is just a pain but none of you have admitted it yet. You might feel that your partner doesn't love you and appreciate you enough, or in the right way. If so, Valentine's Day is mainly a case of keeping up appearances. You go out and buy the obligatory bunch of flowers or the same brand of aftershave yet again. So far so good. But then there is The

Card, the all-important declaration of ever-lasting love. What are you going to write in it? From where to take the words of Thanks and Love You that are not in your heart? Especially if you just had a blazing row the night before, or if you haven't properly talked to each other for months.

If you're really stuck, consider couples therapy. It's usually easier to talk openly with another, a neutral person present. A good couples therapist will not take sides; they will support both partners to express themselves and to be heard by each other. They will suggest new, more constructive ways of communicating, and provide a space within which both partners can feel safe, respected and understood.

But until then; if you would consider trying something different, here is a recipe that might be worth a try:

Love
Ingredients:

Kindness, generosity, gratitude, respect, warmth, a smile or two, talking and chatting, a sense of humour, forgiveness, self-confidence, self-respect, the willingness to be responsible for your own happiness. And here is what you do with it: Thank your partner for something – big or small – at least once every day. Tell them frequently how well they are doing, how lovely they look, how grateful you are to them for doing the cooking and washing, for looking after the car, for doing all the boring paper work, for taking the children to school, or for whatever good you see in them.

If you can't see much good at first, keep looking. Make them a cup of tea when they come home tired. Make them feel welcome in your life. Let them feel that they are good enough as they are. Let them be free. Let them BE. If all this is not coming from your heart at first, just try it as an experiment. All that goes round comes round. *Give first* what you are longing for, or: All you need to do is to love. Try it for a week and see how it goes. You might be in for a surprise!

INNER GROWTH

"The privilege of a lifetime is to become who you truly are."

Carl Gustav Jung

58

Forgiveness

When do we need to forgive? When do we need to ask for forgiveness? Are some things unforgivable? – While thinking about forgiveness I realise what a complex issue this is.

Sometimes we feel betrayed or hurt by other people, or we have hurt or betrayed others and feel the need to ask for forgiveness because we want to put things right. Sometimes this may be enough; by acknowledging that we have done wrong, the other person may feel understood in their feelings, and forgiveness happens spontaneously. This is the aim of reconciliation processes, for example if the victim and the perpetrator of a crime meet, talk openly, and the perpetrator apologises. This process can be healing for both parties; the perpetrators take responsibility for their actions, and the victims feel that their hurt gets acknowledged and appreciated.

But is it always that easy? What is forgiveness? –

It's got something to do with ceasing to be angry or resentful towards somebody. Which means that we were blaming them for doing wrong. They apologise, and we forgive them. Sounds quite straight forward, doesn't it? – Let's assume that somebody lied to you; you feel betrayed and angry or hurt. What does it take for you to be able to forgive? Are you even willing to forgive, or do you want to hold on to your anger? – Maybe you prefer this because it makes you feel righteous, and it gives you a bitter kind of satisfaction to bring up an incident again and again, to punish the other person or to keep them on their toes.

But did you ever think about why they felt they had to lie to you? Could it be worth looking at the bigger picture: What's going on in your relationship with that person? Are there a lot of unspoken things between the two of you? Why does the other person not trust you enough to tell the truth? Could it be that you have a part in this? – I know, this is challenging. But if you are willing to ask yourself these questions and if you detect your part in the situation, you might not even need to decide to forgive. Forgiveness will just happen, because you have realised that in some way you might have contributed to the state of affairs: You are taking responsibility for your part.

What if the hurt is too deep, the wrong-doing too great? – I think the problem with holding on to anger and hatred is that it keeps us tied to the wrong-doer; we stay focused on *them*, and our wanting to hurt them back instead of focusing on ourselves and our own healing.

Maybe some things are unforgivable. Only you can answer that question for yourself. But, maybe with the help of a therapist, you can take some heat out of it by working through it. There will be scars, but the hurt you experienced will no longer dominate and determine your life.

In my own experience, forgiveness is a process: working through deep wounding takes time. There is no point in deciding to forgive if this means that we just cover up our deep pain, sadness and rage; that's called denial. To work through this hurt with the help of a good therapist will often lead naturally to an inner change, and one day you might find yourself feeling okay, or even, to your own surprise, feeling compassion for the person who hurt you. This might happen because you realise in your heart that what they did to you wasn't your fault, wasn't about you; it was about them, their own life-story and their destructive choices. Working through hurt and anger will set us free and enable us to live our life instead of allowing it to be destroyed by constantly focusing on the wrong-doer. This can only be achieved by facing our deepest, most painful emotions instead of avoiding and repressing them. This takes courage, but can bring real liberation and inner peace.

Some hurt, like for example rape, goes so deep that we will always be scarred by it. No-one will ever expect you to forgive rape or any form of sexual abuse, and if they do, tell them where to go. But to work through the hurt, the fear, the rage, with the help of a good therapist who will witness your pain and be your companion while you face up to it, might enable you eventually to heal, at least in some ways, and to break through to a new lease of life. Sometimes it's not about forgiveness at all; it's about claiming back ownership of yourself and your life.

59

Goodbye Loneliness

Feeling lonely and being alone are not the same thing. A lot of people suffer from loneliness, maybe because they live on their own and wish for a companion. Many feel lonely even in a relationship, or in a crowd. Loneliness seems to be one of the major problems in our fragmented culture. We live anonymous lives even in the middle of a community. We may take part in all kinds of activities but are keeping up appearances and are not really connecting with others on a deeper, more authentic level.

The real cause for loneliness is, in my view, the lacking connection to ourselves. – Well, how can that be? you may say. How can I not be connected with myself? And what does that mean anyway? – It has something to do with the way we grow up and with the culture we live in. We learn to bury "unacceptable" emotions – unacceptable to parents or society, like anger, sadness or inner pain. The advice we often get is: Just get on with it, just get over it. If we're not connected to ourselves, we won't be able to connect with others as well. We might wait for others to come to us, instead of finding ways to reach out and make connections. It might not even occur to us that we could.

If we try to "get over it", it is like stepping *over* ourselves and ignoring the part of us that is suffering. That's what makes us lonely; this is how we lose connection with ourselves. In good therapy we can learn new ways of dealing with emotions. Instead of ignoring them, we can learn to acknowledge them and to understand what they are telling us. Maybe they say to us: Your relationship is not satisfactory; you need to do something about it. Or: You're in the wrong job; this is not right for you, and you need to make some changes. Or: You're not standing up for yourself; you don't say what you really think or feel, and blame others instead for not understanding you. Or: You didn't get what you needed or you were mistreated when you grew up, and this wound is still affecting you today, hidden away and ignored. Do something about it. Reach out!

We need to start to pay attention, and stop ignoring the things that are sabotaging our lives. –

Once we start to work through these issues, we can learn to get to know ourselves, to be true to ourselves, to be reunited with ourselves, and to connect with others. That's when loneliness disappears. Then we can be alone and happy in our own company. "Alone" comes from "all one". We can be at one with ourselves, at peace, and this has the great by-product that it makes us much more able to relate in an honest and healthy way to others. Then the choice is not to either be lonely, or to live in a relationship full of drama (or silence). Then we will be able to be alone (all-one), and content, or with somebody, and content. You will be able to enjoy your own company *and* the company of others.

60

Hidden Treasure

We all want to be happy. Most of us work incredibly hard in order to achieve at least something as close to happiness as possible. Often we believe that, if we create a neat and tidy life, then we will be happy. We try to live "in the light", in the positive, and we make huge efforts to eliminate the "the dark", the negative, or what we see as that, from our lives.

The problem is that the more we stand in the light, the bigger a shadow we cast behind us, where we can't/won't see. Maybe we feel the need to create a certain image of ourselves: This is the person I want to be; this is how I want to be seen. We don't want to see the dark side of ourselves, nor do we want others to see it. It's not that, what we judge as "bad", is bad in reality – for example, being "selfish", angry, hateful, being brilliant(!), being different from the norm, having needs, being unhappy when we feel we should be happy with what we have etc. We all have valid reasons for whatever we feel; the question is what we do with these feelings.

The main thing is, to acknowledge them. If we pretend that we don't feel them, we push them away from us, into the shadows. We throw them "out of the house" for being unacceptable and dangerous; we send them into exile: "This is NOT who I am!" But the more we push them away, the more they will push back. They keep knocking on the door, louder and louder; they need to be heard! If we keep ignoring them, we might get depressed and anxious without knowing why. If we try to be somebody we are not, we create a split in our psyche; a gap opens up between the image we create of ourselves and the person we are in reality, and that gap will fill up with anger, depression, panic attacks and/or anxiety.

Paradoxically, the part of ourselves that we fear and reject most, is often the best part of us. Someone might say: I'm so angry all the time, and I hate myself for it! I don't want to be this angry, nasty person! – Later, for example in therapy, they might discover that they're so angry because they always adapt to others, and don't live the way they need to, according to their true inner nature. Their anger tries to save them by not leaving them in peace, by keeping on knocking on the door and saying: You're not true to yourself! You're denying yourself what you really need! Usually there is wonderful treasure hidden in the parts of ourselves that we hate most. If we open the door of our soul and let them back in, the treasure will be unearthed and revealed. You are allowed to blossom and shine as who you *really* are.

61

Kairos – The Sacred Moment

I used to like making plans. I knew what I wanted, and I made plans and went for it. If my plans didn't work out, I struggled on and tried even harder. I tried to force things the way I wanted them to be, and I was convinced, that I knew how they should be, and what was best. It was hard, to live like this. In fact it was exhausting, and it made me unhappy and frustrated a lot of the time. It never occurred to me, that to let things unfold in their own way, might be a better way to live.

The other day I said to my wise husband: "Do you remember when I always made plans, and that I was angry with you, when you said that you didn't believe in plans?" – He just smiled. – At that time, I was convinced that, if I would stop making great plans and forcing things in the "right" direction, everything would fall apart, and things would drift aimlessly. I had no trust in life, in this mysterious force that lives within us; the spirit of life, that none of us can grasp. I felt like an island, disconnected from this great force that some call the "Divine", a power far greater than ourselves. Things only changed for me when I realised, that the "Divine", whatever it may be, might be something that lives *within* me, not "out there", separate from me, and that this inner part of me, the Inner Self, might have plans for me that were far better than my own, self-willed, narrow-minded ones.

Slowly I learned to trust, and to get out of the way, to let things unfold in their own time. Now I have ideas instead of plans, and I sit with them and see what happens. Sometimes they have no substance and dissolve into nothing. Sometimes I sit with them for a long time without doing anything about them – until I find myself doing something about them. Suddenly something happens that inspires me and jolts me into action. And looking back, the timing was always perfect.

"Kairos". This is a Greek word, an ancient concept that means: the right, the sacred, moment or time. Kairos is concerned with the *quality* of time, not the quantity. It's a bit like being pregnant: Something grows and ripens inside, in the dark. It can't be hastened; the child will be born when it's ready. Ideas will manifest in the material world when they're ready. Now I know deep in my heart, that the right things will happen at the right time, when they're ready, when I'm ready. This doesn't mean that I'm just sitting around doing nothing. What I mean is, that we need to wait, feel into our idea, ponder it, see whether something deep within us responds and resonates. When things are ready, we might bump into the right person at the right time; we might hear something on the radio, or stumble upon a book that will inspire us.

For example: For several years I knew that I wanted to start running courses and workshops, and I had a room that I wanted to convert into a space for that purpose, but for a long time nothing happened. From time to time I revisited my idea but didn't feel that impulse, that resonance deep within, that would jolt me into action.

Then I went to a trauma workshop in Zurich and was very impressed by it, and by the woman who ran it. At the end of the workshop I *knew* that I wanted to work with this woman and organise a workshop with her in my city. I went home excited, buzzing, and I immediately started with the renovation of my space. That's when I set out to run courses; hers was the first one, and gradually I began to develop and teach my own courses and workshops. *Now* I was ready!

62

Matters Of The Soul

The word "Soul" is not in fashion nowadays; if at all, we say "Psyche" (Greek for breath, life, soul) which *sounds* slightly more scientific and therefore more acceptable. The word "soulful" is even worse; it can sound cheesy in our ears, and maybe makes us cringe a little.

The word "Soul" ("Seele" in German) comes from the Proto-German "Saiwalo", meaning: She who originates from/belongs to the Lake ("Lake" is "See" in German; hence "Seele"). In old Germanic belief systems, the souls of the unborn and the dead existed/resided in the water, which also symbolises emotion, feeling, and the unconscious. Soul means the essence of a person, their emotional energy, their live-giving core. Soul can't really be defined or grasped, but we know when Soul is present, and when it isn't.

Soul and soulfulness contain deep emotion, and

we're not so good with emotions and feelings. (Some people have attempted to categorise the difference between feelings and emotions, but I remain unconvinced. The categories, as they are, seem random, subjective and hair-splitting to me, and for the purpose of this book I chose to ignore them.) We find feelings confusing and unpredictable; they mess up our plans and lists of things to do; they get in the way of rationality, efficiency and achievement. We're obsessed with work, chores and lists, full diaries and timetables. There is no space or time for Soul, for aimlessly ambling along for a bit; for just being, day-dreaming; or to stand and stare...

We feel uncomfortable if we don't know exactly what to do next, and we need to keep running and planning, otherwise uncomfortable *feelings* might surface, and we can't have that! We will do anything in order *not* to feel; we will keep busy and push on mercilessly. We harden ourselves and say that we have no time for that kind of rubbish. We're being good, we're doing all the "right" things. Even meditation, yoga and obsession with health *can* be used, to avoid and repress feelings. Meanwhile we get sad, frustrated, stressed, angry or physically ill, and we wonder why.

Soul needs space to express itself, through

feeling and creativity. If we neglect that part of ourselves, it *will* backfire. If you sit still and let your feelings come, whatever they are, without judging them as good or bad, you are connecting with your Soul. Our relationships become mechanical and soulless (austere, cold, hard, frozen, dead) without proper emotional connection. Our work can feel empty and pointless, soul-destroying; we may earn a living, but we don't have a life. We may get "depressed" (another mechanical word) and think that there is something wrong with us. But maybe there is nothing wrong with us; what's wrong is that we don't listen to our despairing Soul, our core, our essence, that feels crushed, abused or ignored.

Soul is poetry. Soul needs to play in the mud, to mess about with paint, to make music, to roll down a hill, to laugh and be silly, to climb a tree, to watch a bumble bee, or watch the grass grow. Soulfulness contains tenderness, caressing, enthusiasm, excitement, dosing under a tree, loving our work, loving people, giggling with our children, dancing cheek to cheek, singing out loud and free, eating ice cream. Soulfulness also contains sadness when it's time to be sad, and anger when it's time to be angry; it's about being who we are, warts and all, instead of keeping up appearances.

If you're embarrassed by all this, *be embarrassed*, really feel it, notice the dismissive thoughts in your mind, feel the tension in your body as fully as you can. If you do this long enough, the embarrassment will start to dissolve and transform into – presence. Presence with yourself, and everything around you.

63

Positive Thinking Or Honest Thinking

In January, many of us are thinking about New Year's Resolutions: I will do more of this and less of that; I will think more positively and focus on the good stuff in my life. This can be very helpful, and may remind us, that it's often our attitudes, and how we look at things, that make our lives seem good or difficult.

Sometimes it's good to count our blessings, and to give more praise to ourselves and the people around us; it may help us to feel better, and to improve our relationships with others. But, like everything else, positive thinking has at least two sides: If we use it in order to avoid facing up to things that go deeper than just attitudes, then it's like sticking a plaster on a boil; the infection will spread and poison us from inside. If you're very critical and demanding towards *yourself* then it's often a good idea to learn to be kinder to yourself and to tell yourself that you *are* good enough. But if you know in your heart that a situation is wrong, and you're becoming more and more unhappy and desperate, then it's probably not a good idea to try to convince yourself that you just need to think more positively.

It can be very scary to admit to ourselves, that we just can't go on like this, and that something needs to change, like for example recurring problems in relationships. We may feel confused about what's really going on: Is it all my fault? But if not, how can I change things? We may try different approaches in our behaviour or in our conversations, but soon we're back at square one and feel like we're banging our heads against a brick wall.

Maybe what we learned as children about how to live our lives, or how to cope with problems, is now getting in the way and doesn't work anymore. In these situations, positive thinking doesn't do much good. It's the equivalent of sticking our heads in the sand, and trying to ignore that all is not well with the state of affairs. Then it's probably time to get help, to talk to a trusted person or a therapist, to get new input, some guidance, a different point of view.

It's not easy to realise that we all have blind spots. This is especially difficult for people who are generally convinced that they are right, and that it's the others who are the problem. We can't see ourselves objectively; we need feedback from others to get a more realistic picture of ourselves, whether we are very confident or full of self-doubt. It's not really about thinking positively, it's about getting to your truth.

64

True Self – False Self

We all have to find a way to live in this world. For that, we have to adapt to what's generally acceptable, and we all do this to a lesser or greater degree. This adaption starts from the minute we are born. We need our parents or caregivers in order to survive; we are totally dependent on them, and we learn very quickly *how to be,* so that we get the attention we need – in all its forms. Children who don't get enough attention – or not the right kind – can become very difficult in the perception of the parents.

The purpose of being difficult is to at least get some *negative* attention, which is still better than no attention at all. Other children close down, and become self-sufficient very early on. They are often seen as "independent", as if they don't need much attention. In most cases, this is not what the child experiences; it's just less painful to seem independent than having to fight for attention all the time. If we are really lucky, we have parents who will let us be and become who we are by nature. They will look after us and make us feel safe and loved, and they will be strong and clear and warm and also give us clear, firm, and consistent boundaries, which make a child feel safe.

They will be like good gardeners: They will let the plant grow, water and feed it and protect it from danger. They will wait and see who we are, and let us be that. They will not try to force us into a mould, prune and cut, and try to form us in their image. They will offer guidance, but will let us grow to full size. They will not extinguish our excitement, our enthusiasm and curiosity, they will not crush our little hearts that are bursting with love. Then we will be able to be our True Self. If we have to develop a False Self by over-adapting or over-rebelling, then we will get to adulthood without knowing who we are, and what we want and need. Most likely, we will then marry another False Self and: Let the battles begin!

Two people who don't know who they really are, who try to "be normal" and fit in too much, will make an unhappy couple indeed; be that in a dramatic way, by fighting and shouting a lot, or by suffering in silence until they can't take it anymore, or until the day they die, bitter and disappointed in life.

It's never too late to discover your True Self! It's still there, maybe in a dark corner of your soul, waiting for you to come and find it, so that you can heal, and become who you were always meant to be.

65

Your Voice Of Wisdom

Do you hear voices? – I certainly do! I don't mean those voices that for example Joan of Arc heard, voices of Saints, or the voice of God. – Or maybe I do, actually; I haven't decided yet… But let's start with the less spiritual voices, with the ones we all "hear" in our heads. They may be the voices of our parents or teachers or other authority figures, dead or alive, that now live in our minds.

When we grew up, they told us what we are: stupid or lovely, clever or silly, beautiful or ugly, and we believed them. They also told us how we should be as human beings: reasonable, respectable, rational, ambitious. They may have said things like: Life is a struggle! Don't be such a daydreamer! Artists (of any kind) never make a living! You're much better off becoming an accountant or a lawyer! (Nothing wrong with that, if you love what you do!) Money and material safety are *the* important thing! What? You want a job you love? Don't be so stupid! Love never brought the bacon home!

Either we believed all this and succumbed; and today we may be depressed, angry, or we suffer from "free floating anxiety"; we are anxious but don't quite know why; and whatever we do, it doesn't seem to improve the way we feel. Or we may have rebelled against these booming voices, for example by drinking too much, by taking drugs, or by spending too much money.

However, maybe sometimes you hear another, very small, meek voice that says: But can this be all? Isn't there more to life than a job I hate or find boring, or a loveless marriage? Isn't there more than running after money, or trying "to be somebody" in the eyes of others? – Maybe you dream of dark figures or wild animals chasing you, or of the ground under your feet crumbling away (the unconscious trying to tell you that something is going wrong in your life). But then you dismiss all that and tell yourself: Don't be so silly, you have to be realistic! Life is a struggle! And you carry on as well as you can, still suffering from depression, anger or inexplicable anxiety.

It's that part of us with the little, meek voice, that is depressed, exhausted, or anxious, because we don't listen to it. It's the real ME, the wise ME, that is barely alive under that heap of rubble, under the reign of that harsh, dismissive voice, and we may suffer from all kinds of emotional or physical symptoms. The problem is, that we are totally out of balance. We are so focused on our "outer" lives, that we forget to tend to our "inner" world, to that little voice that so desperately wants to be noticed. Once we start to listen to it and take it seriously, depression, anger, anxiety and symptoms usually decrease or disappear entirely. And who knows, maybe strong people like Joan of Arc were so well connected to their Inner Voice of Wisdom, that they knew what needed to be done. I'm not saying that we all should become "Saints" or "Heroes", but we certainly can learn to listen to our own Inner Voice of Wisdom that knows what we need, and what needs to change, so that we can live a more enjoyable, purposeful and contented life.

66

What You See Is What You Get

This statement was used by Minimalist Artists who made art that often looked like nearly nothing, and upset a lot of people, because they felt cheated. People thought that this kind of art was a con and had nothing to do with "real, skilled art". The point of Minimalism, a movement that emerged in New York in the 1960s, was to reduce art to its essence. "What you see is what you get." There was no hidden meaning, nothing to be figured out. It was just what it was.

"What you see is what you get" to me is one of life's greatest secrets. I understand it slightly differently than the Minimalists: We get what we concentrate on. But it's even more than that: In how we perceive the world, we can see who (or how) we are. If I see problems everywhere, ugliness and meanness, it means that I have a strong critical or fearful part in me that concentrates on the negative.

And if I concentrate on the negative, I will attract it. I will be sour in mind and body and get confirmation that I am right, that the world is a bad place, that people are mean, and always out to get me.

So, it depends on what kind of "glasses" I'm wearing, how I perceive the world. If my glasses are dark, the world seems dark. If my glasses are pink, the world seems pink, which might mean that I am a bit naive, gullible, or ignorant; or just in plain denial. If my glasses are clear – or as clear as they can be – I can see all the colours of this world. I can see the good *and* the bad. I can see that I have a choice: I can chose to always "see" (imagine) all the bad stuff that could happen to me or my family, or I can chose to "see" (imagine) how life would be if I had a basic trust in it. Albert Einstein said, "The most important decision we make is whether we believe we live in a friendly or hostile universe."

Imagine how you would feel, if life was good. Imagine how it would feel to be joyful, contented, at peace with yourself a lot of the time. Imagine how you would feel if you had a job you liked, if you had more time to yourself, time to play, to relax, to potter in the garden. Keep imagining it, seeing it before your inner eye, feeling it. If you do this, you will attract it. You will start to see possibilities; helpful things or people will cross your path just when you need them. We are like magnets. We attract what we see, what we expect.

Many people employ this "strategy" to attract material things, money, fame. That's not really how I mean it. Material things alone will not fill the inner emptiness, they alone won't bring us happiness. It goes much deeper than that. Of course we need to have our basic material needs met, but often, once we have achieved that, we get stuck on that level and just amass more of the same. But: It's only stuff! It doesn't nourish our hearts and souls. As humans we need much more than stuff. But it won't just fall into our laps; we have to work for it and do our bit.

We need to be willing to open our minds and thaw our hearts for the possibility that not everybody has bad will towards us, that most people are good people and have good intentions. We can find fault with everything and everyone, or we can ask ourselves why we are so full of fear, and how we can heal that fear. Good Therapy is one possible way of getting help with questioning and changing our view of the world and of people, our old beliefs and outdated attitudes. How our lives pan out, depends to a good part on the colour of our "glasses", on our beliefs and attitudes. But luckily, glasses can be changed, and so can attitudes.

67

Going With The Flow

Things don't always work out the way we want them to. Often we see a straight line in front of us; we make plans and set dates and deadlines... but then life takes a different turn. This can be really frustrating if we fight it, especially for people who aim to control their lives as much as possible, and believe that they *can* control it. We are told that making plans is important, and that we need to work hard on their realisation. We think that we know what's good for us, and that we will get it if we try hard enough.

For example, I had this fixed idea that I needed to own a house, and that owning a house would make me feel safe. But my life didn't develop in that straight line that would ultimately take me to a point where I would be able to buy a house. It took an unfashionably zig-zaggy course, on which I gained a lot of experience in many different areas, but I was never able to buy that house. Today I'm glad it didn't work out that way. For a long time I moved around a lot, and not owning a house saved me a lot of hassle and money, which I invested in myself instead, in learning, travelling, self-development.

There is a saying that I think of a lot: "You may not always get what you want, but you will always get what you need." This may sound provocative or even upsetting for some people who are experiencing hard times right now. I had those experiences too, and they can be really scary. I remember a time when I found myself with no money, no job and nowhere to life, roaming the streets of a city in Switzerland, wondering where I would sleep that night. A day later I had three (!) house keys in my pocket, all belonging to people I didn't even know that well. But I always believed in my ability to cope with difficulties, and to survive (God knows why!) and I think it was this attitude that saved me. I *knew* in my heart that I would find a way through this, and I was willing to do whatever it took, even cleaning toilets, which I then did for quite some time and with undented pride. Somebody had to do it; why *not* me?

What I learned in those uncertain times of my life was, that a lot of people are happy to help others if we let them (and don't exploit their generosity), and that I am able to survive almost anything if I trust that life will look after me. It gave me self-confidence, and trust in the kindness of others, one of my riches that is now more important to me than to own a house that would shackle me and weigh me down.

"You may not always get what you want, but you will always get what you need." My understanding of this phrase: I will always get the challenges I need (and it's up to me to accept or reject these challenges) in order to heal, to grow, to become stronger, more creative, more trusting, more truthful and authentic; to become who I am meant to become according to my true inner nature. The rest will take care of itself.

68

Be A Fool, And Be Free!

Spring is finally here, and isn't it wonderful not to have to wear all those heavy coats and boots anymore? To feel the balmy air on our skin, and to be able to sit in the garden without thick cardigans; to walk barefoot and feel the cool grass under our feet? – Every spring it's the same for me: The first time I feel the lovely air on my bare arms I feel a deep sense of relief. It's as if my body would say: I made it! Once more I have survived a winter! I can relax and start to enjoy myself again.

This may be a sensation that is archaic, that is still alive in the primitive part of our brains which developed when winters were life-threatening, and brought near starvation and the danger of freezing to death. For the body, this danger is now over, and it might want to leap in the air from joy, like young animals do when they express the sheer joy to be alive. Of course most of us are not so close to our wild side any more, we are much too "civilised" to actually do leaps of joy. We are scared to embarrass ourselves, to make fools of ourselves. We suppress those wild impulses and feel that we have to control or even erase them.

We may be able to control our wild impulses with our minds, but the body is mourning. It wants to be wild and free; it wants to play, to throw cartwheels, to woohoo out loud, and roll in the grass. Maybe that's why we drink so much as a nation, because that's the only way we can feel wild and free nowadays, in a distorted way. The body wants to feel the rain on its skin; it wants to sit in an ice-cold river and then warm up in the sun. The body is part of our wild nature; it's the visible, material aspect of our soul. If we deny this wild part of ourselves, if we bind and restrict it, it might express its frustration through depression, anger, aches and pains or even serious illness. If noticed and listen to, it will give us boundless treasure; the soul/body is the source of our life energy, of our joy of life, of creativity and love.

Most of us see the body mainly as a vehicle to move around in, to go to work in, or to run ever faster in order to achieve. But do we do anything that is "wild" in the slightest? Do we even feel our bodies anymore? Are we able to let the inner child express itself, be playful, silly, innocent? Just imagine for a moment what that would feel like.

Go on, make yourself happy. Let yourself be wild again now and then!

Be a fool, and be free!

69

Lots Of Love!

The other day, after we had finished a therapy session, I showed the client to the door. That's when she spontaneously hugged me, and I hugged her back. We'd spent an hour of deep exploration together; we talked and listened; there had been tears, lightbulb moments when some new insight had clicked into place, and even a moment of relieved laughter at the end. She had suffered major trauma some time ago, and I felt moved by her honesty, and compassion towards her pain. The woman felt fragile, but the spirit that lived inside her was still sparkling! I could feel her warmth and generosity of heart.

In the end it's all about love, I thought to myself, while working with her, and I think that's what we both felt when we hugged each other before she left. She later allowed me to tell this little story and said that the hug, the giving and receiving of it, had been as important to her as the therapy session. This made me think: It *is* all about love, isn't it?

Don't we all recognise the difference between work well done, and work well done with love? By love I don't mean a big sentimental outburst or a dramatic expression of affection, and certainly not an inappropriate crossing of boundaries. I mean this: Every time a shop assistant looks me in the eyes, maybe says a few personal words or makes the effort to give me a proper answer to a question, I feel good. Every time somebody opens up to me and connects with me, I feel my willingness to give more. If I do what I do with love, which means that I'm truly connecting with the person in front of me, in whatever situation, the probability that they respond to me likewise is much greater.

Have we lost our ability to connect, to express love? Have we been rejected too many times? Maybe we grew up in a family that didn't "do" approval, affection, warmth and appreciation, and now we don't know how to give it to others. Maybe we feel embarrassed, or when we do express these generous feelings, we feel shame afterwards. Have we been shamed too many times for being open, giving, vulnerable in this positive way? Maybe we seem matter of fact, demanding but not giving, or even cold to others, possibly without even being aware of it. We ask ourselves why others don't respond well to us, why our relationships are difficult, why our needs don't get met. Maybe we are starved of love and affection, and we forget to give to others what we are longing for.

Most importantly: We forget to give approval, affection and appreciation to ourselves. Probably we are as harsh and critical towards ourselves as the people were that raised us (and the same goes for them and their parents, and so on). If we can learn to appreciate ourselves more, then we will be able to appreciate others too. If we can learn to be kinder and more accepting of ourselves, then we can be more tolerant and accepting of others. Whatever I wish to be different in my life, it always starts with Me.

70

The End

Dear Readers,

This is it for now. Thank you so much for reading this book; I hope you've enjoyed it and maybe found some useful ideas in it. What I would like to say to you, here, at the end: Allow yourself to ask for help, advice and support. We're not islands; we're not meant to live in isolation, or to solve all our problems on our own. Some problems can only be solved, or understood in a new way, in relationship with others.

We can't see ourselves from the outside; none of us can. We all need input from others. We often can't see what's really going on because we are in the middle of it. Another person has a different view of us, one that we just can't see from inside ourselves. Isolation, maybe because of shame and embarrassment, is part of the problem, not part of the solution. Sometimes, if we're stuck in the mud, we need someone else to give us a hand, someone who can help us to free ourselves from whatever keeps us in stagnation, so that we can move again. It's not a sign of weakness to need help; on the contrary: It's a sign of sanity and strength to know when we need help, and to be able to ask for it.

To take *responsibility* for ourselves, our feelings, our needs, means *"to respond"* to *ourselves*, and to realise, that we can't change others in order to make ourselves feel better. The world, other people, will never be the way we want them to be. What we can change, is ourselves and our way to live our lives. As long as we blame others for our problems, we're stuck in the mud, powerless. Once we realise what *we* can do to improve our lives, we're free; we then have choices.

This is not easy work, I know, but it's well worth the effort, for your own benefit, and for the benefit of your loved ones!

I wish you all courage, curiosity, an open mind and open heart!
Lots of love,
Judith

Recommended Further Reading:

Robert Bly:
- A little book on the Human Shadow;
HarperCollins, Australia; Reissue edition (1 Jun.
1988)

Robert A. Johnson:
- Balancing Heaven and Earth, Autobiography;
Bravo Ltd (11 Dec. 2000)
- Owning Your Own Shadow; Understanding the
Dark Side of the Psyche Bravo Ltd; Reprinted
edition (17 Feb. 1994)
- Inner Gold; Understanding Psychological
Projection. Chiron Publications (26 July 2017)

Carl Gustav Jung:
- Memories, Dreams, Reflections; Autobiography;
Fontana Press; New edition (6 Mar. 1995)

Thomas Moore:
- Care of the Soul. Piatkus (2 Feb. 2012)
- Dark Nights of the Soul; Piatkus; Digital original
edition (7 Jun. 2012)

Clarissa Pinkola Estes:

- Women who run with the Wolves; Rider; New edition (3 Jun. 1993)

Cheryl Strayed:

- Wild: A journey from Lost to Found; Atlantic Books; Main – Film Tie-in edition (1 Jan. 2015)

Raynor Winn:

- The Salt Path; Penguin; 7 edition (31 Jan. 2019)

Irwin D. Yalom

- The Gift of Therapy; Piatkus; New edition (27 Feb. 2003)
- Love's Executioner; and other Tales of Psychotherapy; Penguin (4 April 2013)
- Momma and the Meaning of Life. Tales of Psychotherapy; Piatkus Books; New edition (25 Aug. 2006)
- Staring at the Sun. Being at Peace with our own Mortality…; Piatkus; 01 edition (3 Mar. 2011)

Eva Maria Zurhorst:

- Love yourself and it doesn't matter who you marry; Hay House Publishers; UK edition (26 April 2007)

Printed in Great Britain
by Amazon

54446852R00147